This is a beautiful, intriguing, and heart-warming story. The humor throughout kept me wondering what would happen next. Madeline Reid, a retired North Carolina teacher

The author provides a very personal account of her childhood in a small North Carolina town during the 40s and 50s. She adeptly allows the reader insight into family and educational relationships, as well as the prevailing social issues of the time period that laid a foundation and influenced her into adulthood. Judett Black, a retired U.S. Department of Justice Investigator

# Chinaberries
## *and* Beyond

### A Teacher's Childhood Journey

Patricia L. Bostic

WESTBOW
P R E S S°
A DIVISION OF THOMAS NELSON
& ZONDERVAN

WestBow Press books may be ordered through booksellers or by contacting:

WestBow Press
A Division of Thomas Nelson & Zondervan
1663 Liberty Drive
Bloomington, IN 47403
www.westbowpress.com
844-714-3454

ISBN: 978-1-5127-8292-9 (sc)
ISBN: 978-1-5127-8293-6 (hc)
ISBN: 978-1-5127-8291-2 (e)

Library of Congress Control Number: 2017905590

Print information available on the last page.

WestBow Press rev. date:  04/07/2022

# DEDICATION

This book is dedicated to my mother, who was kind-hearted, patient, creative, and always a lady.

# INTRODUCTION

I have many fond memories of growing up in the small town of Belmont, North Carolina. I lived in an isolated area of four houses for African Americans. Every two or three years, my mother would give birth, and eventually, there were eight of us—five girls and three boys—in addition to my parents.

I was their fourth child; I was born during World War II. Each of my siblings and I brought an interesting mix to our small dwelling—a three-room house without electricity or running water. Except for our next-door neighbors who were in an identical house, all other families we knew had water and electricity. However, we didn't dwell on what we didn't have. There was a spring in the woods, lots of nature to explore, and plenty of mischief to get into.

My father had wanted to provide us with adequate housing for years, and his victory in that matter was greater than we could have imagined. Our problematic neighbor, Hazel, was a bully, especially toward my mother, who was soft-spoken and easy going. We barely escaped Hazel's wrath when my family moved from crude to luxury.

In our segregated society, our family's emphasis was on home, church, and school. My older siblings attended Catholic school for several years, and we were all students at Reid High School for blacks for grades one through twelve. I was a smart but timid student during my early years. Later, I found a lot to giggle about when I became popular in high school. Although I had considered myself shy, I realized it was mostly around boys.

My story will take you through my special family memories as well as my church and school experiences and the fun times. My father emphasized education in our house; I knew I was somehow going to college. I chose North Carolina College at Durham (North Carolina Central University). This part of my memoir ends when my brother's car was packed with my things and ready to drive me there. Part 2, *He's Got Me Covered: A Teacher's Personal and Professional Journey, Spiritual Visions, and Revelations*, begins when I arrive on NCC's campus.

# Chapter 1

## HOUSE TO HOUSE

One pleasant afternoon when I was playing outside near Daddy, who was eating pinto beans and onions, he called me over. "Tricie Ann, when you were born, I got a furlough from Fort Bragg to come home. Maggie and the chaps were staying with Gernie and Pete because your mama was expecting you. That was during the war, and then I went on to West Germany ..."

I had heard the story of my birth often from Mo (Mother without the "ther") and at least a portion of it once from Daddy. That day, he paused and stared into space as if distracted by something across the pasture.

When he tried to continue, his voice changed. It became sorrowful. It was hard to imagine that he wanted to cry; that made me feel uncomfortable. I looked away. I wondered who or what had caused him such pain. He stopped the story and just ate.

It was 1937 when my parents were married by a priest in the Belmont Abbey Monastery. Daddy was twenty, and Mo was eighteen; their personalities were as different as sunshine and rain. She was easygoing and soft spoken while he, although kind, had an impatient, outgoing personality.

The Littletons, my father's family, had always lived in Belmont, a small Southern town in Gaston County with numerous cotton mills. Belmont was known as the City of Diversified Textiles. The Littletons were all members of O'Conner's Grove African Methodist Episcopal (AME) Zion Church. My mother's immediate family, the Diggs, lived in Spring Woods, a section in the small nearby township, McAdenville. In contrast to my father's family, they were Catholic and attended church regularly at Belmont Abbey Cathedral.

My parents believed church was where everybody was supposed to be on Sundays. However, several of my mother's immediate family moved to Ohio. A family friend had moved there and convinced one of my mother's sisters to relocate. Another sister followed, and ultimately, my grandmother settled there.

An old photograph shows my parents standing, smiling, arms by their sides and staring into the camera at the edge of a field. Daddy, Nathaniel Littleton, was of average height and medium build; he was several inches taller than Mo. He and his family all had dark-brown skin, while Mo, Margaret Diggs Littleton, and her family all had very light complexions. She was slender and of average height. In the photo, she wore a plain, calf-length, short-sleeved dress with cotton stockings rolled a few inches lower than her dress. Whenever we'd look at the picture, my mother would explain that all the women wore their stockings that way back then. Daddy kept that photograph and other important papers safely locked away in a green metal toolbox.

At the time of my parents' marriage, Daddy had a three-year-old daughter, Dora, whose mother had died shortly after childbirth. She was being reared by her grandmother in another section of Belmont. Mo had wanted to adopt her, but Dora's grandmother wouldn't consent. I don't recall Dora's young life since there are ten years between us. However, my older siblings interacted with her periodically during the years.

Throughout my childhood, my mother talked about way back—her term for life way back when she was growing up. When our family gathered in our hot front room during frightening thunderstorms, Mo's scary, intriguing stories became our ghost tales. Her reminiscing often intertwined with our father's family.

Finding a place to live and to raise a family while making ends meet was a struggle for my parents. There were two cotton mills in North Belmont—Stowe Spinning Company and Acme Spinning Company. A small business area separated the two mills and included a post office and a connected dry goods store, a café, a grocery store, and a furniture store.

Daddy's father died before Daddy had completed his last year of high school; he was forced to work at Stowe Spinning. He was a picker-tender; he operated a machine that picked and cleaned cotton as the beginning of the process of making cloth. Mo made donuts at the Donut Dinette near town. Just off a paved road lined with houses for Stowe Spinning's white workers, the company also maintained three houses for African American workers. The homes were in an isolated spot in a clearing among trees and a thicket.

Daddy lived with his parents and siblings in the first house. Upon marrying my father, Mo left her nearby family home to live with him there. Daddy's older brother, Uncle Ralph, and his wife, Aunt Wilma, lived in the second house. A few months later, Mo's cousin Matt and his wife, Sellie, allowed my parents to rent a room in their home, the last in the row of white houses.

As did the houses for white tenants, each house had a living room, two or three bedrooms, and a kitchen. There was electricity, and a spigot stood high on the back porch. An outside toilet sat at the far edge of the yard. Tenants paid monthly rent based on the total number of rooms—about $2.50 per room—when their checks were cashed at Stowe Mercantile in downtown Belmont. There was no charge for the electricity or water.

In 1938, my oldest sister, Millie, was born in Matt and Sellie's house. Immediately following Millie's birth, Mo had health issues. That necessitated Dr. Edwards and his nurse from nearby Lowell spending most of the day with her until she was out of danger.

Just over a year later, on a sunny fall day, my second sister

3

was born almost under the house. Years of sudsy wash and rinse water splashed from the wooden washtub had apparently rotted the wooden planks of the back porch. One day, Mo stepped outside, fell right through the porch, and landed on the ground under the house. She was stuck in a musty, dark, cramped place where the sun didn't shine. She felt like a giant toad in a nightmare. She hadn't been hurt, but she wanted out of there fast. Dogs had their pups under houses, and she wasn't going to let that happen with her baby.

As she started to crawl out, she saw the brown pant legs of a man approaching the house. Desperate to avoid embarrassment, she scurried on her knees to the front of the house partially shielded by hedges. Inside, she dusted her dress off to greet the unexpected visitor. It turned out to be old man Sloan who, as it turned out, had been visiting my grandparents and decided to go for a stroll.

Later that evening, Mo, Daddy, and some friends gathered to play two card games—drink and smell, and five-up. When one of the guests teased Mo that it looked like a hog had fallen through the back porch, she laughed herself right into labor.

Dr. Edwards paid another visit. Mo's health was fine that time, and so was her second baby girl, Gwen. Whenever our half-sister, Dora, spent time with Daddy and his family, she played with Millie and Gwen.

In early summer, Matt and Sellie moved out, so Daddy, a mill employee, could have rented the entire house. Unfortunately, he made the foolish decision to drive his Model T while drinking. He had a young errand boy in the car. He led the police on a wild chase through downtown Belmont, ended up in jail overnight, and lost his driver's license and his mill job. Worst of all, he was forced to relinquish his housing rights. That was the harsh consequence for any employee caught drunk or jailed for any reason.

The only other available house in the area for an African American family was a crude, unpainted, three-room dwelling on the other side of the Acme Spinning Company, a cotton mill. One side of a section of graveled road—Cason Street, which the family called Acme Road since it was adjacent to the mill—was lined with small white houses for white mill tenants. As if hidden in a valley, the isolated section for African American tenants was downhill behind those houses after a small wooded area. Traveling by car there was a bumpy experience. The curved, sparsely graveled road had large, embedded rocks. We called the road the car way or the car road.

We had to drive over a crosstie bridge, constructed with the same type of crossties used on train tracks, to get to a short graveled driveway that ended in a small parking area for a couple of cars. There, two white mill houses faced each other in a flat section separated by an uphill path and a large, red-clay ditch.

Up the hilly path and to the left stood an enormous white oak, its leaves like millions of waving green hands. Beyond a strip of wild-grass backyard sat a small, unpainted, three-room house just as natural as an old tree. It had no back door. The house was propped up with a stack of mortared bricks on each corner and along the middle where the ground was exposed. A brick chimney centered the sloping roof with a gable facing the house next door.

At the front, two long, flat rock steps led to the small porch. It was flanked by a smokehouse on the left and single door on the right that led into the kitchen. One small mullion window faced the front, while the other two rooms had windows on each of two walls. Inside, the white paint on narrow, tongue-and-groove bead board walls and ceilings had faded. The only way to enter and leave the other rooms was through a plain wooden door. Unlike the mill houses, there was no electricity or spigot there, but there was a practically hidden, stone-covered spring about a quarter of a mile in the woods. An outhouse was down a path away from the back of the house. Daddy paid a farmer, Mr. Shoemaker, owner of the house and adjacent vast pasture, $6 per month for rent.

A lone, towering chinaberry tree sat on a slope out front and to the right of the grassy yard, where the pasture was the dominant scenery. The house and the identical one next to it faced away from each other as if they were being punished. Trees and shrubs obscured a second pasture the elderly Dexter couple owned. A small, red-clay yard, called the clean place, and a grassy area separated the connecting properties. That was the best my parents with two young girls could do. Daddy got a job in another mill to support his small family.

Mo and Daddy got to know the neighbors in the two mill houses at the bottom of the hill. Miss Beulah Jackson, her husband, Mr. Otis, and several children lived on the left. Miss Emma and her husband, childless, lived on the right. But a much closer relationship developed with the couple next door. Mr. Frazier and Miss Delphine were in their late forties and childless. He was a friendly, medium-brown-skinned man with small eyes and even teeth. He immediately tried to make Mo's life a little easier by offering to shorten her trips to the spring. Standing on his porch in faded bibbed overalls and a cotton shirt with sleeves rolled to his elbows, he insisted right off that she go through their yard. He didn't mind if she would be walking directly past their open kitchen window. It made no sense for her to carry her two-gallon water buckets all the way around the outer edge of his yard. Mo at first protested, but Mr. Frazier assured her she'd be glad for that shortcut by the time she got back from the spring.

Mo thanked him and rushed to get to the spring and back before her two young children awoke. Only the dire need for water forced her to take such a chance. After just a few days in the house, Daddy had left without checking to see if the water buckets were full. Breathless and eager to return to the children, Mo raced to and from the spring with two heavy buckets, one on each side. Her fast walk became a switching, running gait. Water splashed on her cotton dress and over the pair of worn slides she had created by cutting the straps off the backs of old summer shoes.

Regretfully, such trips to the spring would play a tedious role in her life. She went there in harsh winter months and during a pregnancy with her third child. It was inevitable that her labor pains would intensify in those woods. One day, she found herself struggling to reach the house with a single bucket of water. Walking slowly, one hand supporting her stomach, she paused briefly by Mr. Frazier's toilet, a common resting spot out of the woods. She finally made it home to relax on a mahogany upholstered chair, the big chair. In warm or hot weather, all windows and the main door were left open during the day. Through them, she heard a familiar voice, Miss Flossie's.

After Grandma Littleton, Daddy's mother, had died, Miss Flossie, a longtime family acquaintance, moved into her house, the first house in the Stowe Spinning Mill's African American section. That day was Miss Flossie's visiting day, and she'd walked about two miles to my parents' current neighborhood. She was wearing a printed apron over a cotton dress with small flowers on it. Her large, high hips yanked it slightly up in the back. Miss Flossie greeted Mo's neighbors at the bottom of the hill. Her gray-and black-streaked kinky hair pulled back in a freshly braided bun was barely visible around the fraying brim of her straw hat.

Visitors to the area were infrequent but always welcome, especially those without transportation; they'd taken the time and energy to walk down the rugged path from Acme Road to the crosstie bridge. Thick vegetation and a small grove of mostly deciduous trees, wild hickory nut, beech, maple, oak, and dogwood separated the path from the graveled roadway. She had a brief conversation with the women at the bottom of the hill; they said their loud, cheerful good-byes.

Mo saw Miss Flossie wiping sweat from her dark-brown forehead with her apron. Her very hefty legs toiled up the hill by the red-clay ditch. She heard her say, "Gotta git on up yonder ta check on Maggie. Gotta see how she's comin' 'long," not caring if she was in earshot of the women she'd just left.

Mo welcomed those last words as she sat bracing herself for her next labor pain. She could hear Miss Flossie struggling. Breathing heavily after cresting the hill, she passed the side window before approaching the front door. Inside, there was no time for the woman to sit and catch her breath. As soon as Miss Flossie saw

Mo, she immediately yelled for Miss Beulah, who was experienced in delivering babies. My brother, Rich, was born that late summer evening in '42.

"Well, Maggie, ya got you a nice big boy, already looking like Nat." Miss Beulah was a tall, light-skinned woman with hair freshly done in several short, nappy plaits. She always had a big smile. Like Miss Flossie, she was a good bit more than pleasantly plump. Her bottom lip was tightly stuffed with Sweet Society snuff. "Ya know," she said, savoring the thought, "he'd be mighty proud having a boy this time."

Mo was fine and happy, and Daddy soon arrived to discover he had fathered his first son. He was so delighted it was as if he'd brought the baby home with him from work. However, since their marriage, ups and downs in their life together had been like an unpredictable, fast, roller-coaster ride. There was joy, housing issues, and babies accumulating within the household. Like on that fast ride, my parents just couldn't get off when they wanted; the attendant would have to let them off. Unfortunately, it wasn't yet their time as marital challenges prevailed.

## Chapter 2

### WAR AND SEPARATION

As a fact of life, particularly in the south, African Americans weren't allowed to sit in cafés, drugstores, or any business to eat ice cream or a sandwich or drink a soda. They couldn't enjoy water from a fountain or even use a restroom unless it was a separate one. Despite this, Belmont was a charming town with a peaceful, laid-back lifestyle. African Americans were socially connected to each other. Except for business, we lived our lives separate from the whites but always interacting with each other.

Numerous relatives on both my parents' sides of our family lived in Belmont, and we'd see most of them at church. Mo especially felt close to Aunt Lydia, her mother's sister, and Cou'n Nancy (we always said Cou'n instead of Cousin), who was related to us on my father's side. But Mo and Daddy still had their personal issues. As the sole provider, Daddy was gone all day while Mo tended three children and handled all household needs alone.

She was sick and tired of carrying water from the spring every day. Plus, she always had to find a time when Miss Delphine could watch the children so she could made a quick trip or two for water regardless of the weather. During the frigid winter months, she also had to carry in enough coal and wood from piles on the far side of the house. Mo had to keep the house warm with the wood she also cooked with daily. She needed a break; she needed a change that would make life easier for a while, and she didn't see that happening while they lived in that house. She was fed up.

Mo often recounted what happened next. There was hardly ever extra money for anything, so Aunt Lydia and Cou'n Nancy supplied all her needs to catch a train to Ohio. Several of Mo's siblings and mother had moved there years earlier. She'd take her three young children, Millie, Gwen, and Rich, who was about sixteen months old.

Like all her close family, Mo had dark-brown, curly hair that she often wore in a pompadour, the rest hanging down her back. For this special but troublesome day, she wore a simple hat as she would when going to church or town. She embellished her thin, arched eyebrows with a touch of Maybelline to enhance her brown eyes. Her high cheekbones balanced out her elongated face and the prominent, straight nose most of her siblings and mother had. It was early January; she put red lipstick on her thin lips. She had considered leaving many times before, but she was determined to go that time. She refused to wait for spring weather. While Daddy was at work oblivious to her plans, Mo took the children and left.

On the train, Mo had to stand; she gave the only available seat near her to her children. Although the girls didn't look like twins, they were dressed that way in clothes sewn by Mo as they often were. Millie was dark skinned and had very dark eyebrows and thick hair; Gwen was medium brown and had thinner eyebrows and hair. Mo had plaited (we never said "braided") their hair in a common style, one plait in the top and two divided in the middle behind. She adorned their front, top plaits with white satin ribbons tied in a bow. They and Rich were dressed warmly for the cold Ohio winter.

Several passengers in the aisles were clinging to the corner of the seat tops to steady themselves. They held a few items in their hands or in cotton sacks slung over their shoulders. Mo was relieved just to be on the train going as far away as she could to cloud Belmont memories. Many thoughts raced through her mind as she stood and

11

watched her children safely sleeping next to her. Pondering her future without their father, she wondered how she would manage. Mo was completely engrossed in such thoughts when a young, fashionably dressed, and attractively made-up white woman tapped her arm. "Ma'am, here, please take my seat." She squeezed into the aisle.

"Oh, thank you," Mo responded, "But I'll be all right. At least my children have a seat."

"Here, take my coat and spread it over them. It's a bit drafty." The polite stranger smiled again as she handed Mo her coat.

Mo couldn't believe what was happening. She'd never expected a high-class white woman to be so genuinely kind and persistent. She was appreciative. The woman's long mink coat kept the children warm while they slept. Mo was thankful for her seat as well.

The many remaining hours she spent on the train allowed Mo time to consider everything about her marriage. She recalled the countless times she'd heard the train whistle blow along the tracks at Acme Mill. If only she could hitch a ride and get away. Above all, she wanted Daddy to be sensitive and understanding of the hardship he could've prevented his family from suffering. She needed time away to lose herself in the midst of her sisters and brothers and their families. They had electricity, indoor plumbing, and lots of help with the children. Until that day, Mo had never questioned her bravery in fulfilling her dreams. The train was not turning back, and neither was she.

For a while, Belmont was history. But it wasn't long before Daddy learned from someone at the barbershop where Mo had gone. He sent her a letter reassuring her of his love for her and their children. He pleaded for her return and promised big changes. He boarded the train to Ohio to bring his family home. Mo's journey was over. They returned to Belmont, where Daddy tried to be a better husband and father, not just a hardworking provider.

However, it seemed that all over the world, tremendous, unexpected changes were underway. And Daddy had no control over them.

World War II had begun a few years earlier. The uncertainty and uneasiness that swept the country affected our little town of Belmont. Many men were drafted into the army, and in late 1943, it was Daddy's turn. He dreaded leaving his family. He became more affectionate and attentive than ever. He and Mo often talked about her plans for the day, the children, and his promise to write often. When Daddy smiled, his high cheeks puffed up, his broad nose turned slightly up, and his brown eyes contrasted with his skin. His black, kinky, soft hair and medium mustache that he kept neatly trimmed accented his wide, thin lips. Daddy always kissed Mo good-bye when he left for work. His most special form of affection was to gently cup her face with one hand (or both if he wasn't holding his brimmed hat) and kiss her tenderly on the lips. She accepted those kisses bashfully.

In January 1944, Daddy traveled to Fort Bragg, North Carolina. Not long after, Mo discovered another child would soon deserve his love; she was several months pregnant with me. Although she feared Daddy might never return, she felt strong and confident. After all, she'd had lots of practice caring for their children alone.

As her pregnancy progressed, however, Mo worried about getting the help she'd need. Consequently, she accepted Uncle Pete's— Aunt Lydia's brother—offer for her and the children to share their modest home. Aunt Gernie, his wife, had insisted. They lived in McAdenville, where Mo had grown up with her eight siblings.

Back then, many people believed babies were likely to be born during a full moon. Therefore, during the summer of 1944, Daddy left Fort Bragg to come home. Unfortunately, he came too soon. I was born a week later in the African American hospital in Charlotte, the state's largest city. After Mo mentioned Grandma Littleton's middle name, Ann, a white nurse, suggested the name Patricia Ann. Mo liked the two names together, and that's who I became. Immediately, Daddy obtained a furlough to retrieve the two of us from the hospital and visit his growing family.

One afternoon several days after Daddy left, Mo settled down with her new baby and assumed her young children were safe outside. Aunt Gernie noticed Millie nonchalantly giving Rich, nearly two years old, dippers of water from the porch shelf. He twitched and whined between gulps. Alerted that something wasn't right, Mo spotted an old, rusty can of Red Devil Lye that had been left out after Uncle Pete had cleaned the shed. Neither he nor Aunt Gernie was used to having children around. Evidently, one of them had pried the can open, and Gwen had fed it to Rich.

Mo and Aunt Gernie were frantic. They crammed butter into Rich's mouth followed by water and sweet milk directly from the bottle. When Rich showed no improvement, Aunt Gernie rushed him downtown to Dr. Walters in their old pickup truck. Rich was lucky, she was told. The butter probably saved his throat and stomach from the burning lye.

Hearing the good news, Mo was relieved but felt Gwen needed to be punished. With her own body still healing from childbirth, she asked Aunt Gernie to spank Gwen. My aunt agreed reluctantly because the child wasn't yet four, too young to be aware of the lye's harmfulness. Neither Mo nor Aunt Gernie could understand why throughout the spanking Gwen yelled out, "Thank you! Thank you! Thank you!" Never able to explain why she had been so grateful, Gwen was teased about that over the years.

When I was about six weeks old, Mo returned home with her four children and a guitar Uncle Pete had given her. Daddy's sister, Thelma, moved in to help her. Daddy sent a handsome picture of himself in his army uniform from West Germany. It was a side view as he stood straight, arms by his side, turning slightly to face the camera. In an accompanying letter, Daddy shared his military experiences of hauling troops, equipment, and military supplies including ammunition at night. Mo was excited to hear from him. However, she was disturbed when she read that whites mistreated her husband and other blacks.

Mo had a picture of her first three children. Near the end of summer, she caught the city bus to downtown Belmont to have a color photograph made with me in her arms. "You and your baby will make a wonderful picture," the white photographer said. Mo was flattered and held me high near her shoulder, gripping me with one arm. I was wearing a thin, white, short-sleeved dress that exposed my cotton diaper and plump, light-brown thighs. My pink hat had white ribbons tied in a bow under my chin, and my small hand was resting on Mo's large one. She wore a crisp, white, short-sleeved blouse with a pointed collar under a bluish-gray and white-flowered vest. Her hair was in a pompadour; the rest hung loosely down her back. Mo faced the camera while I looked in the opposite direction.

The photographer displayed the large original in his studio window as advertisement. He gave Mo a small copy, my only baby photograph, free of charge. She had never known an African American's picture to be displayed in public. She thanked him profusely.

In October 1945, the war ended, and Daddy was honorably discharged after serving in Rhineland. He received the Europe–Africa–Middle East Theater (EAMET) Campaign Medal for serving in Germany, two bronze service stars, and a good conduct medal. Unfortunately, Daddy left a racially segregated army to return to a racially segregated America.

Mo would reminisce about the popular song "Sentimental Journey" written by Bud Green, Les Brown, and Ben Homer and sung by Doris Day. Reminding her of her train trip to Ohio, she enjoyed listening to it on their battery-powered radio and often singing along.

Gonna take a sentimental journey,
Gonna set my heart at ease.
Gonna make a sentimental journey,
To renew old memories.

When we were old enough to understand, Mo often told her Ohio trip story, particularly the train ride. Like a reminder, she

15

explained there were many kind white people; some chose not to call African Americans horrible, degrading names. And if we ever had such an experience, Mo told us to ignore it: "Don't say anything back." She always concluded the story by emphasizing the stranger on the train was a real lady, but she couldn't tell by just looking at her. "I never would've thought that white lady would give me her seat," she said, "much less use her big, expensive fur coat to cover my children."

## Chapter 3

### SHARING THE HOUSE

Though Daddy was often restless and in a rush, he always found time to attend O'Conner's Grove Church on Sunday mornings. Mo and we children attended Belmont Abbey Cathedral, where my older siblings and I had been baptized. However, I was too young to realize my parents and older siblings attended different churches.

In late fall of 1946, we learned it wouldn't be long before their fifth child would be baptized at the abbey too. I was a little more than two when Cassie was born at home. She was named after Mo's mother, Grandma Cass, Aunt Lydia's sister, and the only grandparent I was fortunate enough to have known.

Just over a year later, lots of snow was forecast for Christmas Day. Mo always wanted our yard and under the house to be as clean as the inside without any unsightly trash to distract from the anticipated beauty. Inside, the family talked about Santa Claus. My older siblings said he flew in a sleigh pulled by reindeer. He would, they promised, come down the chimney while we slept. Though in hindsight, our Easy Morning heater's stovepipe was connected to it and always hot that time of year.

I'd turned three by the time I recalled seeing pictures of Santa on the walls of our dry goods store and downtown; he was a plump white man with lots of white curly hair, a beard, and a red and white suit and hat with a wide black belt and black boots. I believed as I'd been told. If we were good, he'd bring us things such as a baby doll, other toys, and candy for me and something for my siblings too.

On Christmas Day, my older siblings and I, wrapped in coats and dragging blankets, went onto the porch to enter the kitchen through its only door. That's when I saw the deep, blinding snow and the wide tracks that must've been made by Santa Claus's sleigh. Inside was just as cold as outside. There were lots of unwrapped presents—dolls, aluminum tea sets, a red wagon, and other toys. Piles of red apples, oranges, and tangerines and a variety of nuts and candy had been placed on chairs.

Back in the house, the heater warmed our multipurpose living and bedroom. There, Cassie, who had learned to walk, and I played with our new toys. I tried to squeeze fresh orange juice into the teacups for our dolls and us to drink. We ate oranges, tangerines, and orange-slice candy and sucked on peppermint sticks that melted quickly in our mouths.

That was a time of being afraid of the boogeyman, and I was sometimes teased by my older siblings, "The boogeyman's gonna get you!" That was a common threat that would provoke frightened reactions as well as smiles and laughter. If I were a good girl, they said he wouldn't get me; other times, those words were just a tease that had nothing to do with my behavior. Though I didn't know exactly how to picture such a thing, the growling, scary face of the boogeyman I imagined is a strong memory of my childhood.

Also, fresh, round coconuts that Mo cracked open for her special Christmas cake were scary; no one had to tease me or say anything about them. They looked like heads with eyes and skimpy hair—mysterious and almost human.

Inevitably, the new year brought changes. The most important came when Mo took Millie, Gwen, and Rich out of the Catholic school they attended and enrolled them in Reid High School, the all African American school for grades one through twelve in Belmont. After considerable discussion, my parents decided that one church and one school were best for their family. By that fall, the whole family had joined Daddy at O'Conner's Grove AME.

While my siblings were in school, Cassie and I played in the warm main room. The red-hot heater's pipes extended over several feet of the slightly worn, floral linoleum. The middle pipe, so thin it looked as if it might burst, had two elbow connections. One was low, extending near the wall, and the other continued up and disappeared under the fireboard. A poking iron and small ash shovel sat nearby in an old water bucket, and a foot tub of coal and a pile of wood were ready to replenish the dying fire. Mo placed a couple of ladder-back chairs turned on their sides around the pipes to protect us—her young children and crawling babies. Clothes, especially denim overalls, that didn't dry on the clothesline in cold weather, were spread over the chairs. Sometimes, those chairs became a train under which Cassie and I played.

Our mother had responsibilities inside and out especially in the summer, but she kept an eye on us as she moved back and forth. That year, she tended a small garden she'd started along the path to our toilet near our backyard. She grew green beans, tomatoes, okra, and several rows of corn. To Mo's delight, Rich planted cornbread in our front yard near her flowers hoping to yield ears of corn; it didn't work. On the other hand, Mo's corn nearly blocked our view of our toilet, and sometimes, I ran through the stalks for fun, dodging an occasional black snake that liked the path and garden too.

When the soil became hard and dry, the garden ended. The food had shown up on our kitchen table during the summer and early fall, but the garden never returned. Maybe babies replaced it.

On the other side of the path to the toilet near the pasture, we had numerous chickens in a lot, but they were all gone before winter. My parents decided against raising them, and the lot was dismantled. We had a few hogs in a secluded, smelly pen just outside Miss Dexter's pasture close to the outer edge of Mr. Frazier's yard. To feed them, Millie, Gwen, and sometimes Rich carried slop in an old bucket from our house. Squealing like crazy, their little hooves carrying fat bodies, the pigs raced toward the trough. Like our garden and chickens, they wouldn't always be there; a few hams soon hung in our smokehouse.

For several years, Mo's sister, Katrina, Trina for short, had lived in Ohio with her three children. During that summer, when she wanted a fresh start with her family, she decided to return to Belmont, where she had numerous close relatives; it had been her home.

Aunt Trina had a young daughter, Rachael, Cassie's age, and two sons, Ben, about my age, and Leroy, a little older. Until they could obtain housing near the school, my parents welcomed them and made space for them in our small house. Mo told her sister to make herself at home, a common, friendly gesture, and Daddy agreed. Aunt Trina often sang "A-Tisket, A-Tasket" as she helped clean the house.

We had lots of fun with our cousins. A favorite game was having the older children push us younger ones in a large, discarded bin with casters. Mr. Otis, our neighbor behind us, had brought it home from the mill and gave it to us to play with. The sides towered over our heads so we couldn't see where we were going as we bumped over wild grass, red clay, and old, fallen chinaberries.

One day, I followed Rich, Millie, Gwen, and my two older cousins to the flat area down by the spring and branch. My sisters carried our two water buckets to fill and take back to the house, but no one was rushing. Instead, we lingered by the branch having fun and singing a funny song in which I struggled to participate. According to the lyrics, one night when the sky was blue, something unusual happened: a scream was heard when a woman was hit by an awful thing flying through the air. The highly unlikely situation was what made the song so comical. We sang as loudly as we could. Far away in the woods, it didn't matter how rowdy we were; we yelled and laughed hilariously with each recitation. That is up until Mo appeared at the top of the hill by the huge oak tree. Disapproving of the song's lyrics, she was furious.

"Stop singing that song right now, you hear me! Y'all know better that that!"

We stopped immediately. We filled the long-awaited water buckets and rushed to the house. Once there, we had a shock. When had Daddy come home from visiting his sister, Aunt Thelma? She lived close to downtown Belmont, but on his day off work, Daddy's time at home was unpredictable. Gwen was especially surprised to see him; her screaming the loudest got her in trouble. This was a hot-bottom day for her to remember—Daddy used his belt a couple of times across her hips. Though Mo didn't approve of the lyrics, she thought Daddy had overreacted. Gwen and the rest of us were just having silly fun. Besides, we weren't in public; we were in the woods. Nevertheless, we knew if we ever had the urge to sing that song again, we'd have to whisper it.

Our cousins soon moved out, but we all remembered that comical song and their fun visit.

## Chapter 4

# THE PUDDLE—GRADE 1

One winter day, a ray of sunlight edged its way through the cracks along the opening side of our main wooden door. There was no lock, just a loose, tarnished latch. But I felt protected as long as Mo was there, and she was most of the time.

In addition to sunlight, cold air flowed through that door as we went in and out. We needed water from the spring. On our porch, we kept some in a bucket and a foot tub that would ice over in the winter. Wash tubs filled our kitchen and made a mess on washday. Coal, chunks of cut wood, and kindling had to be brought in to supply the wood stove and heater. The ashes had to be shoveled into a bucket and taken out to the ash pile.

The main room was quiet except for the sound of hot coals popping in the heater and Grady Cole speaking over our radio on the mahogany dresser. His husky, laid-back voice made it sound as if he had all day to talk. The country songs I heard on our radio became a part of me. I examined the glass tubes in back but could never figure out how Grady Cole and other tiny people talked, laughed, and sang inside.

Just prior to the spring of 1949, Carl was born in our house; he was the second sibling after me. With two parents and six children, the family was growing, but the house wasn't.

Occasionally, Daddy's younger brother, Ed Littleton, walked over from the Stowe Spinning area where he lived with their other brother, Uncle Ralph, and Ralph's wife, Aunt Wilma. Desiring a change in scenery, he seemed to enjoy visiting our family as much as we liked seeing him.

In early spring, relishing the sun on our faces despite a chill in the air, Cassie and I sat in upside down ladder-back chairs we'd propped against the side of the house. We grew excited whenever we saw Uncle Ed come up the hill. For some reason, it was acceptable for us to call him Ed; maybe it was due to his small build and playful personality. He was so funny; he'd often say things and make weird sounds that made us laugh. He could rev like a motorcycle or cluck like a chicken. That day, he chatted with Mo as she did various chores while Carl slept. When he left, outside was quiet again—just the sun, the birds, and us.

With Cassie or alone, I found comfort in sitting idle and sucking my bottom lip while fondling the soft folds of skin I made in my neck. I'm not sure when that habit started, but it was ongoing and Daddy didn't like it.

"Tricie Ann, take that lip out o' your mouth!" That's what he called me when he meant business. He didn't just say Tricie as Mo and Rich did or Tricia as my other siblings did. But his words weren't very harsh. I kept sucking my lip except in his presence or if I had something more interesting to do. Losing my two front teeth didn't even stop me. The tooth fairy left me a dime for each one. But eating one of Mr. Frazier's tart apples became difficult without those teeth. I had to ask one of my siblings with front teeth to start my apple.

Plants seemed to flourish wherever dishwater landed after being dumped or slung out the kitchen window. Mo found time to enhance the front of our unpainted, wooden house during early summer by planting colorful flowers such as tall zinnias and four-o'-clocks. They were shorter with trumpet-shaped flowers that opened at four each afternoon. Both plants continuously bloomed in white and bright colors from late spring through early fall.

Once, Gwen was playing with the small, black seeds and stuck one in her ear; she became afraid. Mo discovered the seed while cleaning her ears and consulted Miss Beulah and Dr. Walters. He recommended pouring sweet oil into the ear to loosen the seed. It came out just fine.

Miss Emma and Miss Beulah had zinnias in their front flowerbeds too. My family could see them as they passed by on their way to the grocery store or the bus stop. (Anywhere we went in nearby civilization, we had to go back and forth up the hill between their houses.) Since Miss Beulah had just four children and Miss Emma was childless, they were different from my mother. While their husbands worked at the mill, the two women often chatted with each other from their front porches. Occasionally, Mo would take part in their talk as she passed. They almost never visited us, though, so they didn't see the beautiful results of Mo's labor, our colorful flowers. And with her numerous responsibilities, Mo rarely had time for lengthy conversation. Those neighbors probably considered her the mother with all those children and a large mutt named Brownie.

In summer, the heat made it difficult to keep flies out of the house because we had the front door and windows open. We had tugged at the blinds, pulled back the curtains, and filled the window to see who was coming up the hill, so our ragged, unsightly screens were worthless. Mo eventually removed them. Any food in the kitchen, especially a blackberry cobbler on which a fly could blend in, had to be well covered. Sleeping babies would be covered with a thin net tent propped up by chairs.

In July 1950, I turned six. The hot months led to many changes, and I became increasingly apprehensive as Mo tried to prepare me for first grade. I wasn't prepared to be among a huge crowd of people I didn't know. My older siblings would be in their own classes. *What if I got lost?* I worried. Other than family, the only time I was around lots of people was at church, and even then, it was mostly relatives.

One day, I watched Mo kneading dough for biscuits on the

pullout counter on our white, free-standing, Hoosier cabinet. We children called her rolling pin the dough roller. Almost every meal, breakfast and supper, we had hot biscuits or occasionally cornbread. And any leftover biscuits or dough was always used. Uneaten biscuits became bread pudding; my favorite was chocolate. Also, Mo made old-fashioned cinnamon toast with butter, sugar, cinnamon, canned milk, and maybe a little vanilla. Leftover dough became sourdough biscuits or flat cake (rolled dough not cut into biscuits). Any extra dough was used to make piecrust or sticky with butter, cinnamon, and sugar. Cassie and I baked dough in jelly lids. It tasted awful, like a mixture of burned rubber and paint!

But that day, there was no extra dough for us. Mo rapidly cut out biscuits with a slightly bent metal cutter. She shaped the last bit of dough into a biscuit, filled the blackened baking pan with them, and placed it into the piping hot oven. "Tricie, you'll be riding the big school bus tomorrow with Rich, Millie, and Gwen," she said.

"Will their classroom be next to mine?" I needed her to say yes.

"Rich's will. Millie and Gwen are older. Their classrooms are in another building." She paused and glanced up as she scraped excess flour from the cabinet into her dough bowl. "Your teacher's gonna help you in your classroom. Like Rich, you'll get used to it."

Those were essentially Mo's no-nonsense, comforting words. She took a quick peek at the biscuits in the oven.

We all took our baths at night in a tin washtub or had wash-ups in our porcelain wash pan. In either case, Daddy insisted the bar of Lifebuoy soap should never be left in the water to soften and go to waste. We found privacy in our parents' closed-door bedroom; we hid our private parts, which Cassie and I referred to as "down below." We bathed behind a chair with some type of cover thrown over it. Though Cassie wasn't ready for school yet, we took baths and prepared for bed together. We found white cotton slips we used as nightgowns and white cotton bloomers in our chest of drawers. After saying our prayers, we were ready for bed.

But I was anxious. I knew my morning would be very different from Cassie's. Physically, I was slender and of average height for first grade, but I still wasn't ready socially. On her Singer pedal sewing machine, Mo had made me a plaid dress of primary colors and white that was contrasted by a white collar. It had a wide plaid sash tied in a bow in the back and hanging over a full gathered skirt. On the first day of school, I wore new, brown oxford shoes with white socks as if I were going to church. Mo combed my dusty-brown, lightly straightened hair and made three plaits. She tied a white satin bow to my top plait. Having slept squeezed between the warmth of most of my siblings, I ate hot oatmeal with sugar and diluted evaporated milk from our icebox. I loved oatmeal hot or cold. I grabbed my new, plaid book satchel filled with supplies and hurried down the path behind our house with my older siblings and Brownie. We ducked under low-hanging branches of the big tree as we called it at the lower edge of our backyard.

Near the parking area, the Jacksons' old pickup truck was backed uphill parallel to the far side of their house. There was no sign of schoolchildren. Millie and Gwen had talked about how the Jackson children somehow always managed to be ahead of them. We all walked single file up the path. On that day, however, my main concern was Millie's, Gwen's, and Rich's reassurances that my school experience would be all right.

As we walked speedily over the bridge and up the path to Acme Road, Rich shooed Brownie home. He wagged his tail and stared at Rich as if he wanted to linger, but he turned around and reluctantly obeyed. We passed the baseball field where white teams played. We following the path across the railroad tracks, crossed the main street, and stood under a large willow oak. The Jackson children were there waiting. Though a couple of them were about my age, they were mama children and almost never played with Cassie and me; they stayed close to their family.

The yellow, antiquated, secondhand bus arrived already filled with children, many Millie's and Gwen's ages. I hadn't seen them at church; they were strangers to me. The experience was intimidating.

The old bus jerked desperately to make a right turn at the stop sign near Belmont Abbey College. Minutes too soon, we arrived at the school.

The brownish, redbrick elementary section of Reid High housed two classrooms each for first through third grades. The buses lined up along the curb and unloaded at the first building on the main street. The long outside wall was filled with tall, mullioned windows with dingy, beige shades all evenly rolled halfway up. The corridor had dark hardwood floors. An open coat closet had numerous hooks. Inside my classroom, rows of dark wooden desks were connected. Each had a grooved pencil holder on top and flip-up seats. A musty smell of lead pencils and crayons from many little hands of the past filled the air.

My teacher was Miss Cranford, a familiar face; she was my cousin on Daddy's side of the family. I rarely saw her in her neighborhood, but I'd see her in church on Sundays. She was warm and friendly while she worked with us youths at church and as my Sunday school teacher. I was in a small group with mostly cousins. But at Reid High, Miss Cranford was different; she was stern.

As always, my two sources of comfort were church and home. Most of the folks at church were familiar faces if not relatives. At home, Cassie and I played with dolls and did girlie things together, but I also enjoyed following Rich around. He could do lots of things I couldn't; he was my big, brave brother. Like Daddy, Rich wasn't much afraid of anything; he'd take risks occasionally to the limit. He was mischievous too, and that's when he'd get in trouble all by himself.

Knowing Rich was close by at school was comforting. Still, school was a scary place for me for a while, and Mo's reassurance didn't seem to be working. I was timid and cried at intervals during the long day. By midwinter, my distress had declined considerably, but I was still adjusting.

One very cold December day when light frost covered the fallen leaves, after shivering in the cold at the bus stop, we arrived at the elementary building. Inside, I removed my headscarf and heavy coat and hung them in the closet near my classroom. The coat was part of an aqua wool legging set handed down from Millie to Gwen and then to me. My old leggings, though, were new to me. On cold days, it was common for elementary girls to wear denim or corduroy pants under their dresses and remove them in class as their bodies warmed. I was not sure how to remove my thick, wool leggings, so I kept them on.

For devotion, the class stood and sang a song familiar to everyone who attended Reid High. It was the good-morning-to-you song about being in our places with sun-shiny faces to start a new day. After the pledge to the flag and the Lord's Prayer, we sat.

Miss Cranford was slightly plump and had broad, flat hips, just like my father's family, Aunt Thelma and their brothers. A medium-brown woman, she had thin, wavy hair always worn with a part on the side and curled under just above her shoulders. Her eyes were round and small. I disliked when she narrowed them, turning her slightly bushy eyebrows into a *V* and making wrinkles in her forehead. Like all female teachers of that time, she always wore a dress, or skirt, blouse, and sweater combination, or occasionally a skirt and suit jacket.

As Miss Cranford stood at the blackboard that day, I was squirming. The drafty room had become warm, very warm, and I grew increasingly nervous. Finally, my body relaxed against my will, and I felt a warm flow on my seat that wet the tail of my cotton dress. In an effort to stop it, I squeezed my knees together and crossed my legs and ankles tucking them under my seat. The urine came anyway. It trickled down my legs and wet my leggings, socks, and brown oxford shoes. A small puddle formed under my seat. Tears streamed down my face. I knew Miss Cranford would eventually notice, but right then, she continued talking to the class though none of her words registered with me.

I wiped my eyes and the mucous from my nose. I fought back tears and sniffles. Finally, when I could no longer stifle my anxiety,

I broke into loud, uncontrollable crying. In no time, Miss Cranford was at my desk, scolding me.

"Patricia, I know you know better than that! Why didn't you raise your hand if you needed to go to the restroom?" She paused and stared at me. "Sit there and wet your clothes!"

I couldn't answer. I cried louder as the entire class focused on my face and puddle.

"Now what am I going to do with you?" That made me cry out even louder. "I guess you'll just be wet all day."

When I wouldn't stop crying, Miss Cranford got Rich from his classroom as she had done earlier in the year when I cried about something or nothing as it seemed to her. In brown corduroy knickers, Rich stood by my side as if to comfort me and help Miss Cranford decide what to do. Though I had no change in clothing, they helped me remove my shoes first and then my wet leggings. The narrow pants legs had short zippers at the ankles, which made removal even more difficult.

After Rich left and I'd returned to my desk, my classmates continued to stare while I sobbed quietly in my damp seat. But even that was easier than it would have been to interrupt Miss Cranford. During certain times, she had the entire class line up to be led to the restroom. Nature had thrown a monkey wrench into the schedule, and I just hadn't known how to handle it.

I spent the entire school day in smelly, half-dry clothes. While my classmates had sun-shiny faces, I had stormy morning, noon, and evening blues right until I entered our warm, cozy home. A pot of pintos with a hunk of fatback was cooking on the heater as I told my mother about my stressful day. It was as if she imagined it happening to her. Her warm voice and comforting words soon made everything all right. She made a large pan of cornbread, and I found some leftover oatmeal to hold me till supper.

Fortunately, I became less timid and more sociable as the school year drew to a close.

Second Grade

MRS. FALLS

30

## Chapter 5

# SCHOOL AND CHURCH—GRADE 2

In Sunday school, Miss Cranford taught us about Jesus and how great He was. Church attendance was important; not having anything to wear or something being wrong with our shoes was not a good excuse. Unless one of us was indeed sick, we all went. Our clothes weren't supposed to matter in church anyway, though we were always neat and clean. Every stitch was ironed and our shoes polished on Saturday evening. That included white dress shoes in summer, brown oxfords needing oxblood shoe polish in winter, or black shoes. We took baths on Saturday night. If my sisters' or my hair needed straightening for any special occasion, that was done on Saturday nights as well.

On Sunday morning while we dressed, we listened to church services on the radio. That day was different from the others. We walked about two miles to Sunday school in pleasant weather or piled into the family car, a black Ford sedan, if not.

Every June at O' Conner's Grove AME, Miss Cranford oversaw Children's Day, a special day to honor children. Miss Cranford gave us verses to learn depending on our ages and abilities. Almost every child who could talk participated. On Children's Day in 1951, all the girls dressed in frilly white dresses, and the boys wore white shirts and pants and sported recent haircuts. The girls wore white polished shoes or black patent-leather slippers. Our hair was straightened with fewer plaits than usual or left loose with curls formed overnight by twisted, brown paper hair rollers. Regardless of the style, satin ribbons enhanced our hair. The year before, Cassie had almost cut her big toe off after stepping barefooted on a piece of glass. She was unable to participate. But that year, there she stood very proud and ready to recite her speech.

"Happy Children's Day to you, and you, and you!" Cassie pointed to different sections of the congregation while everyone smiled and applauded.

Uncle Ralph had a daughter a little older than Cassie. The verse she recited very fast in one breath and tone was memorable: "I am just a little girl I don't have much to say but I can say one thing happy Shillren's Day!" Everyone laughed and applauded loudly as she rushed to her seat.

By that time, Miss Cranford had learned how easy it was for me to memorize verses, and I was given more than the few lines I'd had for previous speeches. Although I was nervous, I knew everyone present and felt proud after giving my recitation. My life's focus had become school as well as church and home.

One Saturday night, Mo prepared for a special occasion: we were having the preacher for Sunday dinner. Reverend Smith was a dynamic speaker; the congregation respected him highly. He came with his wife and three girls, who were close in age to Rich, Cassie, and me. I'd admired their small, attractive, friendly family in church. That Sunday, the girls wore similar, store-bought, pastel dresses with full skirts and wide sashes. Their feet were adorned with fancy patent-leather slippers and thin white church socks. Ribbons enhanced their straightened hair.

On Sundays, we usually had various combinations of food for dinner: macaroni and cheese or potato salad, creamed potatoes or rice, canned sugar peas or green beans, roasted or stewed beef and gravy, and fried or stewed chicken. But with company coming, Mo couldn't go wrong with fried chicken, potato salad, green beans, sliced fresh tomatoes, and store-bought rolls. Dessert was store-bought pound cake with canned fruit cocktail. Mo didn't trust making cakes in our wood stove. Cassie and I had rolled lemons to make them juicy for fresh lemonade served in jelly glasses. We didn't ask for the fried chicken gizzard or what we called the toughie; that would have been bad manners in front of our guests and embarrassing to Mo.

Once when our cousins on my father's side were eating Sunday dinner with us, Mo and some of us found humor in one of the young girl's question: "Ma, we gon' eat agin when we go home?" Mo knew what it was like when children spoke as if they'd never been taught. (Although my family doesn't recall the answer to the question, we still laugh about it.)

While some of us waited, others squeezed around the table to eat with our guests. Afterward, most of us, including Millie and Gwen, took the girls on an adventure. They were not used to a house or surrounding areas like ours and were fascinated by the pasture out front. We took them on the red-clay roadway between the two pastures and watched Miss Dexter's light-brown cows grazing near the barbed-wire fence. Unripe persimmons hung from a tree; the cows, my siblings, and I would eat them later in the fall.

We chatted and strolled to the edge of the woods. The girls were in awe of the unique setting. The sun was shining through maples and dogwoods, two of my favorite kinds of trees. I liked the maples' smooth bark and prettily shaped, bright-green leaves; the dogwoods had a rough textured bark but delicate white flowers in the spring.

The preacher's daughters were in their fancy clothes. We took turns on Rich's bicycle, which I had learned to ride by taking off from our rock front step. Then we walked through the woods to the spring; they couldn't believe we had to carry water such a long distance to our house.

Before the family left, each girl had a turn on our tire swing, which was attached to one of our chinaberry tree's largest branches. Our lifestyle was so different from theirs and that of the other families we knew (except for the one next door), but our visitors were captivated by it. Although they'd dressed differently from us, they accepted us. They were fancy; we were plain. What a fun day. The girls were as amazing to us as our surroundings were to them.

Whether going to church, town, or staying home washing clothes, my mother always wore a dress. The first time I saw her in pants was the day of the summer church family picnic. She wore light-blue pedal pushers with a white cotton blouse hanging loose. Mo was still a real lady though. Each family had packed lunches in big, cardboard boxes. We took a bus that left in the dark early one Sunday morning. As we neared our destination in the North Carolina mountains, everyone unloaded at different intervals for sightseeing. At one lookout point without a railing, one church member snatched Rich from the mountain's edge. Some said if he had slipped, he'd have been surely eaten by bears. Mo scolded him for leaving her side. She said to the onlookers, "I don't know what I'd do if anything that terrible ever happened to one of my children." Mo realized the picnic was a potentially dangerous family outing. Daddy seemed to have left keeping track of us to her. Still, we all enjoyed the picturesque scenery. The views were much more interesting than the pasture at home.

I sat by the window on the long trip home. After everyone had settled down, Cassie sang "Good Night Irene" and her favorite, "I Love You a Bushel and a Peck." When she sang the line, "and a hug around the neck!" she flashed a big smile. She liked singing those songs at home too.

It was soon dark. Many slept while I watched the big, glowing moon through the trees' dark silhouettes. Then, it was intriguing to see clearly the entire full moon over Mr. Shoemaker's pasture. That moon had followed me all the way home. That was the most beautiful part of the trip.

As I went to and from the grocery store with Millie and Gwen, I got to know the four white Radcliff girls who lived in the mill house for white tenants next to our path. Three of the girls had funny nicknames—Bunny, Dumpling, and Pootsy. When my sisters lingered to chat, I played with the younger girls on their old, abandoned pickup that sat in the clearing between our path and our car way. Each girl had long blond or light-brown hair they didn't seem to care about brushing. They were skinny and went barefoot. The younger ones went topless, wearing only shorts, the same as my younger siblings and me on hot summer days. With the girls and a younger brother too, their family was big like ours and just as carefree.

Even then, I realized a whole other mysterious world existed between the Littletons and the Radcliffs, one I didn't understand. Society's unbreakable wall, one we could see only partially through, eliminated any close, open relationship. The Radcliff girls and we were so alike but so different; they were white and we were African American.

Cassie, Rich, and I spent much of the summer exploring the woods. When the branch overflowed after a hard rain, we'd play in it pretending to swim. Too soon, Gwen or Millie remembered the buckets of water had to get back to the house, or we saw a water moccasin and got out. We were used to seeing snakes, especially the long green ones that slithered on the branches of matching green trees along the path to the spring. The black ones preferred the path's edge to our toilet when the weeds hadn't been cut down with our grass slinger. None of us liked snakes, but they were always spotted where we had to travel repeatedly.

A short distance from the spring's branch was another branch. After crossing it, an uphill path through the woods led to a garbage dump, trash piles, and the back of Miss Cranford's home. Some of her relatives lived in the area. As we walked through the woods, my siblings and I ate plump currant berries, wild plums, and blackberries or licked the saltiness from wild sumac we called salty dogs. We roamed all day and returned home sweaty and hungry. Mo was always relieved when we arrived. To tide us over until supper, we often found snacks for ourselves: sometimes cold biscuits with jelly, apple butter, molasses, or Karo syrup with butter stirred in, something we also ate for breakfast with hot biscuits and liver mush.

On a Sunday, another hot summer activity was going to Tucker's Grove Camp Meeting in Lincoln County, which was west of Gaston. The event attracted crowds of unfamiliar African Americans, and there was a lot of preaching, singing, and food. Mo considered this family trip safer than going to the mountains. Regardless, being shy, I was uncomfortable, and the gnats, flies, and dust didn't help matters. However, many appeared to enjoy the outing.

Sundays after church were often quiet and boring. There was no extra work to be done, no mopping and waxing, washing clothes, or cutting the grass. Sunday was the Sabbath Day, and we were to keep it holy, though Daddy said if the ox was in the ditch, we needed to get it out.

One lovely day, Mo suggested we have a picnic in the woods. We carried dinner along with dishes, utensils, and an old bedspread through the back edge of the pasture. We stopped when we came to a clearing near our familiar creek. The sun was barely peeking through; we laid our spread over a thin bed of pine needles and ate macaroni and cheese, fried chicken, green beans, and red, ripened tomatoes, a gift from Miss Emma's garden.

Tomatoes were one of my favorite summertime foods. Mo sliced them with our only sharp kitchen tool, a big butcher knife. We drank dippers of spring water from the bucket since Gwen had used the knife to stir the gallon jar of grape Kool-Aid. (When the jar broke, there was excitement and a big, sticky mess all over the kitchen floor.) Normally, I played only with Rich and Cassie. That day was delightful, wonderful, and different with Mo and our older siblings around. Some of us caught tadpoles and let our feet dangle in the cool creek water. Too soon it ended, but banana pudding awaited us at home.

The picnic was different from running and playing and thus skinning knees and elbows that Mo flooded with hydrogen peroxide.

Sometimes, a coating of bismuth violet or mercurochrome, a red antiseptic, was used to treat our injuries. Wearing shorts, we were colorfully spotted. However, Mo said our sores needed to heal before July's rainy dog days because sores took longer to heal then.

On other lonesome but pleasant Sunday afternoons, the family, including Mo, headed to the street that ran by Miss Cranford's house and the abbey. During our boredom, just seeing people in moving cars connected us with civilization. We walked through the pasture or along the red-clay roadway. Near our destination, a barbed-wire fence with an electric wire across the top enclosed a pasture for a milk cow. Roaming the woods with Cassie and Rich, I had been shocked when touching that wire. After laughing at me, Rich persuaded Cassie to touch it, prompting another burst of laughter. That cow wasn't going anywhere with a jolt like that on her big belly. Mo's stomach had grown big too.

Traffic to and from an adjoining small township north of the abbey was light. The family, chatting and laughing, lingered along the street in the wide, sandy driveway of a large, one-story white house. It appeared no one was home. Some of my siblings and I played games with passing cars. We claimed them by color or guessed the next one to come around the bend. Before the sun went down, we strolled home.

One day, all of us children had been away from the house. As soon as we got home, we were told to stay outside and play. Daddy had come home early, and Miss Beulah Jackson was getting ready to leave. My youngest brother, Dan, the seventh child, had been born. On that Sunday morning following his birth, Daddy helped out by preparing a special breakfast of pork chops with rice and gravy. While we had pork chops once in a while for supper or on a rare occasion for Sunday dinner, we never had them for breakfast. Filled with excitement and meat, most of us were off to church.

That summer, other interests took us away from home. Millie and Gwen had heard classmates talk at school. They anticipated seeing an African American TV show called the *Amos 'n' Andy*

*Show.* We sometimes listened to *Amos 'n' Andy* over the radio. Then one day, Uncle Ralph and Aunt Wilma invited us to watch it on television in their home. After some coaxing from us, Mo agreed. However, there was to be no sassing, and chores had to be completed in a timely manner. From then on, Rich, Cassie, and I went too to enjoy a couple of hours of the Thursday-night programs. Sometimes, though, we fell asleep. We'd awake and dread the dark, two-mile walk home in the night air. Uncle Ralph never drove us home in his Nash maybe because he had to work at the mill the next morning. Nevertheless, he probably assumed we'd be safe. I don't recall ever seeing anyone out on our way home. All the families in the mill houses appeared settled in for the night.

By fall, I was even looking forward to starting second grade, but that year would be unusual. Daddy had enrolled to complete his senior year of high school. With the GI Bill of Rights for veterans, he'd also attend barbering school in the afternoons. All of us had new book satchels or notebooks and supplies to begin the year, and Daddy had needed books and a few things for himself. Though Cassie and I frequently wore homemade dresses, we had new, store-bought clothes and shoes.

Students from Miss Cranford's class had been assigned to Mrs. Cox. She was a tall, dark- skinned woman with a face as smooth as satin that never shined. Her smile showed her large white teeth and big dimples in her full cheeks. Her straightened black hair was parted on the side, pulled back over her ears, and curled under. She wore black shoes with little heels. Miss Cox was as gentle as a mother away from home. She praised my good work just as Mo did when she checked my report card along with my sisters' and Rich's.

As in first grade, we wrote with fat burgundy pencils without erasers as if we'd never make a mistake. And the class was always in line for something: washing hands, taking nasty little, rubbery cod-liver oil blisters that sometimes burst in our mouths, getting drinks of water, and paying our twenty cents a day for lunch. We stood in line to go to lunch and the restroom. However, if only one of us needed to go, we'd take a shortcut through the adjoining classroom. Crossing the back, we'd politely hold our hand up and ask the teacher up front, "May I pass, please?" The teacher's answer was always, "Yes, you may."

On pleasant days, we lined up to go outside for recess and play games such as Little Sally Walker. With our teacher monitoring, the class formed a large circle, holding hands and walking clockwise while one girl, the Sally Walker, stooped in the center. First, we sang about her sitting in a saucer, rising, and then wiping her weeping eyes. Whoever was Sally stood and wiped her eyes. The class continued walking and singing for her to fly to the east and fly to the west then fly to the one that she loved the best. Sally then whirled around where she stood, covering her eyes with one hand, the other arm outstretched. She pointed to a classmate to replace her.

I don't recall the boys playing Sally, but there were other group games for them and us including I Lost My Pocket Handkerchief. Later, we divided into small groups for jump rope, hopscotch, or our own creative games.

Daddy seemed to be playing a game with me. I saw him at school, but he didn't seem to see me. Occasionally, I caught a glimpse of him in the corridor headed somewhere for older students. Still, he didn't see me. Then he'd leave early for barbering classes only to be seen again at home.

Thanksgiving Day was extremely cold and overcast that year. Mo dressed our baby brother, Dan, in a blue-legging suit she'd made for him, placed a cap on his head, and wrapped him snugly with a blanket. The family, all except for Daddy, walked along the chilly stretch of road from the city bus stop close by the school bus stop. Our trip ended at our cousins', Louisa and Frank's, nice brick house. Mo thought the parade route passed there diagonally across from the abbey.

Cou'n Louisa was a teacher in a nearby town; she was home for Thanksgiving, and the smell of sage and turkey came from the briefly opened door. Hearing the drums in the distance, we all got excited only to learn the parade route went through downtown Belmont. Surprisingly, it was just ending. Having missed Santa Claus in the parade's grand finale, we were all disappointed. Mo was dumbfounded and declared, "I just run out!" That was her usual way of admitting a mistake that was all her fault. She knew nothing else she said would bring the parade along that route that day. The family briefly rested in the warmth of our cousins' living room and headed home.

Mo finished the holiday meal she'd partially prepared that morning including a large, stuffed hen instead of a turkey. After saying the blessing, she stressed how we had so much to be thankful for. Throughout our lives, she reminded us there were so many people worse off than we were. Usually, it was in particular reference to our own dire circumstances and our house's lack of conveniences. Food was always plentiful in our home, but it may not have been what we wanted to eat any one day. I preferred liver mush and canned salmon patties rather than sausage or bacon for breakfast, but Mo taught us to appreciate whatever we had while insisting on good manners. Even on Thanksgiving, we were not to waste food by putting more on our plates than we could eat. The advice was emphasized for Christmas too, as our unrealistic Santa Claus lists were altered. For example, if Rich wanted a bike and a scooter, he couldn't expect both.

After Christmas and into the New Year, there were still lots of leftover fruit and a huge peppermint stick stored in our cold smokehouse. Daddy's old boots and army clothes hung there along with a few hams. Long after the fruit supply was depleted, each day, we stood on the porch in the cold after supper holding out our hands. Mo, sitting in the chilly smokehouse doorway, gave each of us broken chunks of peppermint candy. She ate chocolate-drop candy but warned us it was too sweet and would rot our teeth. When I had a rare one, I enjoyed eating it with English walnuts.

Even without treats, we had riches in our family and the confines of our little house. We always thanked the Lord for our food and other blessings. We never forgot to kneel by our beds to say our prayers and make the sign of the cross before jumping in. Nightly, Cassie, our younger siblings, and I said the prayer "Now I Lay Me Down to Sleep."

*Chapter 6*

# DEATH AND THE SIX-LEGGED DOG

In late spring '52, Uncle Clyde died; that was my first experience with death though I felt closer to his wife, Aunt Lydia. When my family visited, we rarely saw our uncle at home. Most of the time, he was working at the mill or on his way there. Though Daddy was at work in the barbershop, he sent one of his customers in our family car to pick us up so we could attend the wake at Uncle Clyde's home. The small white house was filled with familiar and unfamiliar relatives and visitors. The kitchen overflowed with an assortment of foods enough for Sunday dinner over and over.

In the corner of the small front room, Uncle Clyde's body lay in a casket adorned with fragrant flowers; there were additional arrangements and wreaths throughout the room. Aunt Lydia sat in an upholstered chair solemnly conversing with visitors. Uncle Clyde's large, short-haired dog, restless and confused, lay by the coffin. He whined, occasionally barked, whined again, and climbed repeatedly to the coffin's edge before settling down.

Upon seeing our uncle's body, Millie, who was holding Dan, and Gwen began crying, then Mo. Surprisingly, Rich burst out laughing at them, causing Mo to promise him a whooping. A spooky experience for me, the wake was worse for four-year-old Carl. When he saw the body, he almost went into a spasm. Mo had to rush him to the front porch for fresh air; she caressed and shook him in her arms until he seemed himself again.

When Daddy finally sent our ride to take us home, the man put us out at the bottom of the hill in our usual space. It was already dark. We walked together, climbing the path to our gloomy house. I was scared. At the front rock step, Mo rambled in her pocketbook for a long-stemmed wooden match to light the lamp on the fireboard. Then she kicked the door wide open as if to say, "Is anyone or anything in there that doesn't belong? Come out because we're coming in!"

I had already thought of every ghost tale I had ever heard before we quietly followed Mo in after she lit the lamp. She'd told us about a large woman in a white dress she'd seen standing in the doorway of our house after she first moved in. Mo didn't know who the woman represented or why she was there, but she had never forgotten that.

The tale the family talked about most was of the fearsome Mr. Sam Wilson, who had lived and died in our house. His first and last names were always said together. Mo never said how he died, if he had been sick, or was just very elderly, but his dying in our house was more than I needed to know. Even worse, the constant warmth of the brick chimney that stretched from floor to ceiling on the wall behind our front room heater was connected to Mr. Sam Wilson's ghost. I didn't want to touch that brick even in daylight. Though Mo hadn't seen his ghost, others in Belmont claimed they had. That night especially, I didn't want to remember any of those dead people. I really hoped none would be back.

We were tired from the long evening. After we'd all knelt and said our prayers, my sisters and I climbed into our big bed in the main room. We found our usual spots, sardine style, under the covers. The boys slept in the same room tucked into our red vinyl sofa bed. After saying goodnight, Mo took the lamp into the other room, leaving ours dark and creepy.

Exhausted, we slept until dawn.

Near the end of the school year, I spotted Daddy in the window of the school's upper-level library. I stood in line with my class waiting to enter the cafeteria for lunch. I stared at him hoping he would wave, but he never noticed me. Perhaps he was focused on the upcoming prom, which he planned to attend with his wife before completing his senior year at Reid High. Mo was already busy on her dress. She had bought yards of vibrant pink satin cloth for a flared, long skirt. To hide her collarbone, which she felt was too pronounced, the rounded neck was high. And not wanting to expose her upper arms, she chose short sleeves over sleeveless. Mo felt her arms' curves showed too much evidence of hard work.

On prom night, she wore her hair in a pompadour, the rest hanging down her back. She pinned a pink rose above her ear. Daddy had bought a black suit that fit perfectly. His black dress shoes shone, and his hair was freshly cut and neatly brushed back. Even in everyday clothes, our parents were our prince and princess, but we were not used to seeing them go out together. All dressed up, they were gorgeous.

Daddy blushed through his dark, healthy skin as he smiled for Mo when she appeared before him. Her lipstick blending with her dress against her olive-toned skin, she was indeed a lady, not the hardworking woman Daddy usually saw. His expression said he was proud of his wife, but he was just as handsome as she was beautiful. As we crowded the small back window of our house, we were like the Jackson children who watched our goings and comings. At dusk, we saw our parents go down the hill to an awaiting car and disappear. That was a grand prom night for them, the special, older couple who looked like the queen and king of the ball.

Following the prom, Daddy graduated with excellent grades first from Reid High and then from barbering college. He then completed a barber apprenticeship with the school's janitor, also a barber. In a shop a block from school, the two worked together for years. This made us children proud and happy for another reason:

the shop was convenient for us to get permission from our teachers to go ask Daddy for forgotten lunch or spending money.

Eventually the sole barber in the shop, Daddy had many customers; Fridays and Saturdays were his busiest days. His earnings satisfied our basic needs. Numerous times, though, Mo told us about her hair-cutting dilemma with Daddy: would he cut their boys' hair at home or in the shop? Occasionally, if the shop had been crowded the night before, a customer was allowed to come to our house early on Sunday morning for a haircut. (During the summer, I recall Daddy cutting a couple of men's hair on our porch.) When needed, Daddy cut Rich's and Carl's hair at home as well. By that time, their haircuts were long overdue. That didn't concern my brothers, however, not even when Mo jokingly described their hair as looking like little cockleburs.

The first time she complained about the boys' appearance, Daddy agreed to cut their hair. But realizing we'd be late for church, he decided the haircuts could wait. Mo explained it was embarrassing for a barber's children's hair to be unkempt. His always looked good, she said, but he was neglecting his children. Mo didn't like Daddy's response the next time she reminded him how badly my brothers needed a haircut. It was the beginning of a memorable story.

"Bring them to the barbershop this evening," he'd told her. Then he handed her a dollar, which included 10¢ bus fare.

"Nat, you know I have too much to do on Saturdays. This house needs cleaning, and—"

Daddy ignored her, kissed her quickly beside her mouth, and rushed off to the barbershop.

Mo explained her disappointment in his hasty, unreasonable response. Daddy knew Saturday was cleaning and grocery day. She hadn't even made out her grocery list for Rich to take to the store. Then after everything was delivered, she needed to get a head start on Sunday's dinner before making a quick trip to town. And she hadn't yet hemmed Rich's britches for church. To spend time

45

catching the bus to take the boys to the shop would disrupt her day and waste valuable time.

The days had grown shorter, the air was crisp, and the leaves were losing their autumn glow.

Mo relied on her stretchy-band watch for her and the boys to catch the four o'clock city bus. They'd walk to the main street near our school bus stop.

Not used to being home after dark without Mo, the family waited anxiously while caring for young Dan. We'd strained to see through our back window. Finally, after several hours, we were elated to catch sight of them climbing our hill. Mo and the boys entered the house.

Still breathless but relieved to finally be home, Mo told us the shop had been very crowded. And while it was good to rest, she couldn't relax. She had just sat there waiting with Rich and Carl all that time watching Daddy cut hair in his short, white barber jacket. (As a rule, common courtesy, and good business sense, all customers' hair was cut before family.) Mo said she kept checking her watch because it was getting late; she didn't want to miss that last bus, but they had. She looked disgusted knowing it could've been prevented.

Mo continued as she sat on the edge of the bed. She explained that by then, it had gotten dark. After passing O'Conner's Grove and the Esso Filling Station, she decided that with the children, it was safer to take the shortcut through the abbey. At that time of evening, not even one priest was out. It was so dark along the narrow paved roadway that she could barely see. Even the beautiful, heavenly grotto was scary. Mo added that she thought she'd faint in her hot dress. She'd wished she could've taken it off and walked home in her white cotton slip.

Not long before that, an elderly priest had walked from the abbey through the woods to our house to give Mo a box of clothes. In it was a long-sleeved, gray, wool dress with red trim. Its flared skirt was calf-length. The priest had held the dress up to himself, saying in his soft, accented voice, "Dis is for da mudder; it fits like dis." Mo adored that dress. However, the temperature outside was not yet cold enough for her to wear it comfortably.

We stayed focused on Mo, who seemed to want to share all the anxiety she'd felt. She explained that when she'd heard a loud, clanking noise by the garbage cans, she'd picked Carl up and grabbed Rich's hand and ran as fast as they could. When she looked back, she said she could've sworn the six-legged dog was following them. Then it was gone.

Mo's adventure was scary and intriguing. More than once, she had told us how mean old Mr. Ethan was. She'd said there was a coal chute by the college where he used to unload coal. Then, he was killed in a car wreck on the main street Mo concluded, shaking her head in disgust. The rumor was that his ghost, a six-legged dog, had been roaming around there ever since.

We all listened and joked that there wasn't even a thunderstorm, which had been deemed the perfect time for ghost tales. To our surprise, Mo seemed just as upset as she went on to end her barbershop story. It had caused the whole, awful, frightening experience in the first place. She knew Daddy had been a smart student at Reid High, but when he was being blatantly inconsiderate, she'd say he was an educated fool. Mo was adamant with her conclusion. "Nat knew he could've cut his own boys' hair here at the house! That's the last time I'll be taking my chaps to the barbershop!"

With that on that unforgettable Saturday, Mo had gone to her bedroom to remove her attractive dress, the one she'd looked so good in when visiting her husband's shop.

## Chapter 7

# DRAMA AND THE FOUR-LEGGED DOG—GRADE 3

That summer, Rich discovered an Asian pear tree by the edge of Mr. Shoemaker's pasture along the clay roadway. Not knowing the tree's real name, we called the fruit rusty-core pears, and we'd crawl through the snaky weeds to retrieve them. Unripe, they were almost too hard to bite, but later in the fall, they became soft and sweet. The problem was that when school had begun, we sometimes forgot about them.

Several jersey cows and a white-faced bull roamed in the same pasture, so we'd always avoid the sections where they grazed or rested, but they never kept us out of the pasture. We just made sure we didn't get too close to them. Sometimes, they wandered just on the other side of the barbed-wire fence near our yard; that was a safe distance to watch them from.

Once, the bull got out through a section of fence we frequented and had loosened. There he was, standing by our clothesline and staring at Mo. She tried to shoo it away. When that failed, she sent Rich to get Mr. Shoemaker from his farmhouse nearby. All of us children fretted from the porch. We were afraid for Mo, who stood in the yard watching the animal's every move. For the first time, I was afraid to go inside for protection. I was sure something, not someone, could come through the main door and endanger us. Fortunately, Mr. Shoemaker sent a couple of men to capture the bull and mend the fence. That experience was one of the most exciting events of the summer.

That Halloween, for the first time, we had a party and invited the Jackson children. They had never been in our house. They all said they'd come. In preparation, we partly cleared the smokehouse and lit it up dimly with our kerosene lamp. We hung orange and black paper chains. After cleaning a washtub, we filled it with water and several red apples. That night, we took turns bobbing for apples, drank hot cocoa Mo made in a big pot, and ate store-bought sugar cookies and candy corn. It was a memorable gathering.

I became quite bold in Miss Crowder's third-grade classroom. One day, a cute girl sitting in front of me whispered she was going to write a love letter to our school bus driver. He was a high school student old enough to have a big girlfriend. I had often seen him carry her books at the end of the school day. He also walked her to her bus before beginning our route home. Nevertheless, I liked my friend's idea and decided I'd write him too.

Later that evening, when most of the family was busy with homework, I sat by the corner of the dresser. The kerosene lamp was at the other end. I wrote,

Dear Tommy Dunn,
I love you. Do you love me?
Patricia Ann Littleton

I thought of it as a love letter. When I saw my friend during recess the next day, I told her I too had written one. She looked at me as if she'd forgotten about it.

Throughout the day, I anxiously carried the note folded in my plaid book satchel. I couldn't imagine giving it to Tommy Dunn, but that evening, there was an unusual twist of events. The graveled bus lot adjacent to our classroom building was filled with students of various ages—elementary through high school—waiting for buses, one of which had broken down. That wasn't uncommon, but some students always rode the second load to areas just outside Belmont including Gastonia.

In the excitement, I forgot the letter, but when I realized we had to wait a while, I secretly removed it from my satchel. With my back to the crowd, I sat on the grassy slope by the parking lot and playground. Before I could reread it, a brown hand with long, skinny fingers reached over my shoulder and snatched the note.

"Patricia wrote a letter to Tommy Dunn!" shouted Clara, one of my classmates.

Laughing, teasing, she read my letter aloud and repeated, "Patricia wrote a letter to Tommy Dunn!"

"Gimme my letter! Give it to me!" I screamed.

I frantically chased after her crying. Clara was skinny and very fast, but Rich stopped her and snatched the letter back for me. Fortunately, neither Tommy Dunn nor his big girlfriend ever learned of one of the most humiliating experiences of my eight years.

Another time, our school bus broke down on a very cold, overcast, winter morning. My siblings and I waited by the huge, barren willow oak with the Jacksons. We moved about hopping intermittently to warm our bodies. Our teeth clattered as we all shivered in the cold. I was surprised the water in my eyes and the mucous in my nose didn't freeze, and I couldn't understand why my frozen toes didn't break off inside my oxfords. Long, wool coats and headscarves weren't enough.

We saw Daddy's car make a left turn off Acme Road onto our street far down from where we stood to his right. Unfortunately, he was oblivious to our need for a ride as he headed for work. No one talked of returning home; school was too important. It was a good place for learning and being with our classmates, our friends. We did many stimulating activities as one big, organized family. After a long while, the bus finally came.

Like any other winter, if snow was in the forecast, my siblings and I got excited, and sometimes, the forecast was accurate. If we were lucky enough to get a second snow, it was considered cleaner and safer to eat. (I learned much later that the first snow cleared a lot of pollutants from the air.) Daddy usually made snow cream and enjoyed it with us. All he needed was what we had on hand: evaporated milk, a little sugar, and vanilla.

Reid's elementary classes presented a spring operetta near the end of the school year. In preparation, after lunch, students packed the only classroom with a piano for rehearsals. Meanwhile, in the community, women who could sew, including Mo, helped make the colorful costumes. We children were building our self-esteem when and wherever we interacted with others at home, church, or school.

But I knew I'd never be the star of the operetta the way I was at my church with long memorized speeches. It seemed the girls most likely to be selected for leading roles in the operetta were the pretty ones with long, straightened, or naturally curly "good" hair. It also helped if they were neat and wore nice clothes, or were light-skinned, or had relatives who were teachers or prominent members of the community. And even if I'd gotten a leading role, I realized I'd probably run off the stage when I saw the gym overflowing with spectators.

The day of the operetta came. Accompanied by the piano, on stage in the gym, my class sang, "We are little pussy willows" as we made breezy, swaying movements in our pussy willow costumes. Cassie's class sang, "We are little raindrops, falling from the sky. We make pussy willows wake up from their pillows." Rich and the boys in his class were leaping frogs and had to jump and croak across the stage in skimpy green frog suits. Many children became colorful, spring flowers, making the operetta a beautiful, memorable, musical event.

On one of the hottest July days, my family and I attended a Littleton family reunion held on spacious church grounds under huge willow oaks in nearby Gastonia. We looked our best just as we always did for church. Gwen had learned to straighten hair and had taken that task over from Mo. Despite our living conditions, Mo wanted her children to be well taken care of. She made sure that her girls' hair was at the very least neatly plaited and that her boys had regular haircuts. Cassie and I wore pretty dresses Mo had made, white church shoes, and hot, thin socks. I longed to be barefooted; my feet craved fresh air and the feel of cool dirt and grass.

Never had I seen such a large gathering of Littletons, most of whom I'd never met maybe because they didn't attend our church. I was fascinated by one aging, frail cousin who was short with dark, smooth skin like Aunt Thelma's but with a much smaller frame. Wearing a neatly ironed cotton dress with small, colorful flowers and a buttoned front, she was slightly bent and walked slowly with a wooden cane. I watched as she briefly removed her wide-brimmed straw hat to fan her face. Her coarse gray hair was pulled back in a thick plait secured with bobby pins. She caught my eye and slowly approached where I stood near the food-covered tables that held lots of desserts, mostly homemade cakes and pies. Nearby, a young woman fanned flies with a folded newspaper. Others, including some of my close family, milled about in the area.

"Now whose pretty li'l girl are you with those great big, pretty brown eyes?" the frail woman asked me. She stared at me trying to figure me out. I shyly glanced to see where Cassie and Rich had gone. I was uncomfortable in large crowds of strangers. Not knowing quite what to say, I preferred not to talk. However, it was clear she expected an answer.

"Nat Littleton's," I responded nervously as if she might contradict me.

"Nat Littleton's! Ya don't mean it!" Her high-pitched voice was just as dramatic as the expression on her face. She put all her effort into remembering. "Now, I knowed Richard." She was concentrating. "You must be next to Richard."

Everybody knew Rich or at least had heard about him through Daddy.

"Yes ma'am," I answered, relaxing a little. I was also next to Cassie's age I wanted to add. She and Rich were my two special links, the best of both worlds: a girlie sister two years younger and a daring, mischievous brother two years older.

"Um, um." She was thinking things through. "Well, I'm your Cou'n Tilley, Tilley Mae. Your Daddy's mama used to bring him, Ed, and all of 'em, Thelma, and ..." She hesitated. "... Ralph too to my house on Sundays, um, um." Her dark hand rested on her chin exposing large veins as she continued to reminisce without me.

I never knew Grandma Littleton, but I learned later she had been one of the first students in the first African American elementary school classes held at O'Conner's Grove. Seeing Cou'n Tilley was lost in thought, I eased away to catch up with Millie and Gwen. Both said Daddy had told them about spending lots of time with our cousin when he was a young boy. They and Dora, who was probably somewhere nearby, had all visited Cou'n Tilley before I was born. Millie and Gwen remembered Grandma Littleton too.

For the rest of the day, Cassie and I mostly played with cousins we knew from church, but we warmed up to a few relatives we'd just met before going home. Mother and a woman about her age talked of how relatives unfamiliar to me had died. Overall, the family reunion was a pleasant experience. That's where I fell in love with pound cake, which tasted so much better than our usual Sunday store-bought cake. I'm still in love with it.

Despite limited funds, Mo came up with creative ways to beautify and improve our surroundings. In late spring that year, she dug a large hole in the grass to fit a small washtub between our yard and Mr. Frazier's. She filled it with water and several goldfish she'd bought in town. Once she planted colorful flowers all around it, we had a beautiful new fishpond.

Fish, though, were not the kind of pets Rich wanted. He had found Brownie dead from a gunshot and had been asking for a replacement dog. Finally, Mr. Otis Jackson, the friendly neighbor behind us, gave Rich a goat since his family no longer needed it for milking. That animal tried to eat everything, and Mo eventually said it had to go. But not long after, one of Rich's white friends from the mill village gave him a long-haired brown, white, and black mutt. He was a friendly dog like Brownie, but he was shorter. His long, fuzzy tail wagged most of the time. Rich named him Shaggy.

During the school months, the family was busy, but summer was a time we became reacquainted with one another. This included the younger ones with whom I didn't share common interests. I helped take care of them; we all took care of each other.

Saturday was a busy day in the Acme Mill area; it was filled with excitement and cheering during the mill's occasional afternoon baseball games with all-white teams that drew many white spectators. My family and I knew the game was a whites-only event, and we'd never consider stopping to watch or cheer. In fact, when Cassie and I passed by on the path from the store with grocery bags, I felt uncomfortable as if the spectators' eyes were on us rather than the players.

However, Rich communicated with some of the mill village boys and made friends with several. Sometimes, they explored our woods. He also became close to Mr. Frazier; he spent time with him when he came home for lunch from the mill. The two often chatted while Mr. Frazier shared his bologna sandwiches or Vienna sausages until the one o'clock whistle blew.

Mr. Frazier had numerous chickens that wouldn't stay in the shabby lot near his apple tree; they roamed about in their front yard and ours. When I first saw them, I thought Daddy had gotten us chickens as we'd had years ago, but they were just visiting, clucking and pecking at the ground. The only problem was most of us except Millie went barefooted during the summer. The chickens didn't care if their excretions landed in the bare, red-clay clean place we swept to make our yard look good or to play hopscotch. Sometimes, the excretions dropped on our front, grassy yard or on the path to the spring. The sudden soft, moist feeling between our toes was disgusting.

Sometimes, Miss Delphine came out with breadcrumbs or chicken feed calling, "Come, chick, chick, chick!" She'd spread the feed in their yard, and the little hens and rooster went running and pecking at the ground. Once in a while, Mr. Frazier laid a chicken on a stump in his yard and chopped its head and feet off or wrung its neck. I pitied the chickens; I was happy when we had chicken from the grocery store to fry or stew. They were already dead and cleaned; with each bite, I didn't have to feel sorry for it.

Even as Rich and Mr. Frazier talked, Rich had his eyes on that rooster. One bright, sunny day after thanking Mr. Frazier for lunch and rushing away, he climbed onto the iron bedrail at the foot of our parents' bed. He found a bottle of Daddy's whiskey hidden on top of our dark-brown chifforobe, the tallest piece of furniture we owned and sometimes called a wardrobe.

Rich climbed down, carefully filled a jelly jar lid with whiskey, and returned the bottle to its original spot. He placed the lid on the ground at the corner of Mr. Frazier's house for the rooster and chickens to drink. When the rooster, king of the barnyard, had downed a sufficient amount, it crowed like no other fowl had ever crowed before. Rich laughed and laughed thinking the rooster was drunk as it danced around in a circle flapping its wings and feathers flying. When Mr. Frazier saw his rooster acting crazy and saw Rich in our yard giggling to the point of discomfort, he was certain my brother was behind the mischief. The man was angry.

"Rich!" he yelled. "What did you do to that rooster? I'm gonna tell Maggie on you!" He tromped toward our yard. "You ain't got no business bothering those chickens!"

Mr. Frazier did talk with Mo, but not knowing about the whiskey, he couldn't fully explain his reaction. But she knew how mischievous children could be, especially Rich. Mo reassured him

Rich would explain the situation and be punished if necessary. Her son liked animals, she explained, and it wasn't his nature to get in trouble with them.

When Rich revealed what he had done to the rooster, Mo whipped him with a hickory switch she'd made him get from the shrub near our chinaberry tree. Of course he'd made certain to break it slightly in several places to lessen the pain. He was punished for getting the rooster drunk and for climbing up to reach the whiskey.

I knew how to climb up there too. That's where I had found a brown paper bag of rock candy Daddy had hidden. It was so different from any candy Cassie and I had ever eaten. It was beautiful, almost clear, like crystal clusters that tasted like Daddy's whiskey smelled. But I never got caught.

In spite of his whipping, that wasn't the end of Rich's mischief with the chickens. The summer wasn't quite over when Rich overheard Mr. Frazier talking with his wife. He didn't know what was happening to some of his chickens; his flock was decreasing. Since he didn't discuss the matter with Mo, maybe he underestimated Rich's capabilities and didn't suspect him.

Later, when Rich thought enough time had passed to avoid punishment, he revealed his secret to me. It seemed he had trained Shaggy to chase and catch the chickens and follow him into Miss Dexter's pasture. He'd clean the chickens, wash them in the branch before the cows came, and roast them over a small fire on the slope behind the trees. He gave the dog whatever he couldn't eat. We knew we were not to tell Mo not yet, not ever.

Our small house had the basic necessities along with a few accessories. In the main front room, called the *house*, a colorful linoleum rug covered the wooden floor. A mahogany dresser and chest of drawers flanked one wall, and a large bed filled another. In one corner, a heavily stained whatnot with a few figurines hung opposite a colorful, wooden weather house that looked like a small birdhouse. When sunny weather was predicted, a small girl and boy appeared. Otherwise, a figure resembling a witch in a black raincoat popped out. An eight-by-ten picture of Grandma Cass hung nearby in a narrow wooden frame. However, the dominant framed picture was a large one over our mantel, which we always called the fireboard. It showed a ship atop avocado waves. With the windows propped open, the room was fresh and airy as off-white, lace curtains blew away from the worn venetian blinds.

While we were having fun, most of the time, Mo was quietly working and coming up with ideas for improving our house. Mo liked change; she liked making old things look different, more refreshing, and appealing to the eye. One time, she decided on a tremendous change. Before we'd moved there, our smokehouse had been an add-on where several hams had hung and for storage as there were no closets in our house. But Mo saw the small room as little more than a deteriorating eyesore. While it shared one wall with our main room, the other three attached walls weren't properly secured and therefore weren't as sturdy as the rest of our house. It had been years since we had hogs that provided hams that hung in there. Ultimately, Mo decided to sacrifice storage for a better-looking house.

Our small porch, a tight space through which our large family frequently passed, was closed in by a smokehouse wall and the kitchen wall. Daddy agreed with Mo and arranged for Miss Cranford's brother, who lived near her and worked in home construction, to remove it. Once the job was done, we all liked our old house's new look. The former smokehouse porch section revealed sturdier brown planks compared to the small, weathered, well-used area leading to our front door.

Like Mr. Frazier, we had a long covered porch with a shelf extending to the corner of the house. That's where we sat a bucket of drinking water and a long-handled metal dipper, again like our neighbors. On hot days, we all drank freely from the dipper, which had to be replaced too often. To rectify that problem, we began drinking from a small, sturdy saucepan shaped just like the Big

Dipper. To us, it was just a little pot. One day, we took it to the spring and had a contest to see who could drink the most water. Somebody told, and when Mo found out the reason we had taken so long while she needed water for cooking, she was livid.

While no one enjoyed carrying heavy buckets of water from the spring, sometimes, we had fun there. A few crawfish, large and small, were always on the sandy bottom. Most of the time, they stayed put as we filled our buckets. Sometimes, we caught the crawfish and played with them, eventually leaving them to die surrounded by ants along the spring's path. Once, there were no crawfish; instead, we saw immature mosquitoes we called wiggle tails. The water had become stagnant and unhealthy and therefore undrinkable. Since the spring and branch were surrounded by trees, many fallen leaves had halted the water flow. Therefore, until the spring ran fresh and clear, our family was allowed to get buckets of water from the Jacksons' outdoor spigot. Mr. Frazier used Miss Emma's.

In the summer, in additional to hopscotch or jump rope, Cassie and I played jack rocks and tried to use a paddleball both purchased at Joe Farrington's store. We caught June bugs in daylight, tied string to their legs, and let them fly around on those leashes. We caught lightning bugs, fireflies, at night. At dusk on cool, moonlit evenings, we played games such as Ain't No Bears out Tonight, a kind of hide-and-seek tag. One evening, we were playing Annie, Annie Over taking turns throwing a softball over the roof of our house. At least one of us was in the front yard while the others were on the grassy backyard slope. Someone yelled, "Annie over!" The response was, "Let it come!" If the ball landed short, it bounced hard and rolled on the roof. Mo was furious when she heard the loud noise. Damage to the roof might be expensive to repair, even more than the house was worth. "Stop throwing that ball on the roof right now 'fore you mess around 'n' put a hole in it!" she'd yell from inside. Hardheaded (what we were called when we disobeyed or ignored Mo's warnings), we kept playing but cautiously until the cool evening grew too dark to see the ball.

A safer game was a form of charades that we played inside and out. One of us made shadows against our parents' bedroom window shade while some of us sat in the backyard in the dark. We used objects from the sewing machine such as scissors or spools of thread. We made other shadows with our hands. The game usually continued until we depleted our ideas or were exhausted and needed to prepare for bed.

By the wash place on the far side of our house was an old tree bearing small, freckled peaches. A couple of its large branches reached over the dangerous top edge of our roof. Rich had been warned not to climb it, but he considered it the ultimate challenge. He enjoyed sitting on the high roof and seeing things from a different perspective. One day, Daddy came home and caught him relaxing on the roof's edge eating a peach. Daddy insisted on helping Rich climb down, but knowing he was in trouble, Rich pleaded to get down alone. "I can get down by myself, Daddy. I can get down." He carefully scurried down the tree where Daddy waited with his loosened belt. Rich didn't climb on the roof again. And as soon as the peaches were gone that summer, the tree was cut down.

## Chapter 8

### STORMS AND RAINBOWS

Mr. Ben Mathow, the white policeman, knew my parents and was friendly and respectful to my mother. Over time, he offered her a job doing light ironing in his home on Saturday mornings. Mo obliged since he lived not far from the mill village. Besides, Millie and Gwen were old enough to watch us children for a couple of hours or so.

The thought of earning personal spending money for household items such as new curtains or a replacement for the worn, red-and-white checked oilcloth on our kitchen table appealed to her. She had to heat two heavy irons on our wood stove for ironing. Our ironing board, a padded wooden board covered with a sheet, had to be propped on two ladder-back chairs and held steady by a heavy, rectangular iron weight. She had to test the irons with a touch of a tongue-moistened finger. When one iron cooled down, she put it on the stove and picked up the other. With electricity in their home, ironing for the small Mathow family would be easy.

On a weekday during the summer when I turned nine, Mo took all of us children to visit Cou'n Edna who, like Aunt Gernie and Uncle Pete, lived near Mo's old home place. We left early in the day when it was still cool. The plan was to arrive around noon and return home before dark. Mo knew Cou'n Edna couldn't feed all of us; she too had quite a few children. Instead, we planned to have a picnic in the woods along the way. We'd take the shortcut because it was too hot and too long a distance to walk along the main streets. The older children took turns carrying a lunch box of bologna sandwiches with iceberg lettuce and Duke's Relish. We traveled by Acme and the Stowe Spinning Mill areas and passed the isolated African American section where Uncle Ralph lived.

Well into the woods, we stopped in a wide clearing where pine trees flanked the path. When we continued after lunch, Mo could barely decipher the trail since it was no longer used as often as when she'd lived at home. Entire sections were covered with weeds and wild plum trees that we picked fruit off of along our way. Mo repeatedly warned us to watch for snakes.

Soon, we came upon an old, brown, rotting shack that I'd visited once when I'd been at Uncle Ralph's house. Mo explained that his sister, Thelma, had once needed a place to stay and that little house was all he'd been able to offer. Aunt Trina had shared the house with her briefly before I was born.

We traveled in intermittent sunlight and stopped periodically to rest. Mo didn't want to waste any time, though; we had a good distance to go. Was she teasing when she said we might have to run back to that old shack if a storm came up? That got us moving fast; no one liked the sound of a storm or the idea of seeking shelter in the shack.

We were exhausted and damp with perspiration when we came to a desolate, weedy field that looked almost as big as Mr. Shoemaker's pasture. Mo was elated; we were almost there!

When we finally arrived at our cousin's small white house, we were offered cool spring water from jelly jars. It took a while to warm up to Cou'n Edna's children. Though we occasionally saw them at school and several were about our ages, we had no real personal relationships with them. And even though they had electricity, their mother still used a washboard like Mo's to scrub clothes in a washtub outside. While we were there, two older girls rinsed some in a creek as they straddled the large, smooth rocks and let sudsy water flow downstream. I had never seen anything like it. We lingered in the shade by the creek conversing mostly with our siblings.

Soon, we were playing hopscotch and taking turns riding an old, rusty bicycle along the same dirt roads Mo had ridden on as a child, all of us finally having fun. After a serving of blackberry cobbler and more spring water, it was time to leave. The sky had turned ominous. Mo always said it was bad manners to eat and run, but Cou'n Edna didn't want us to get caught in a storm either. Besides that, Mo knew if we waited, we might get lost in the dark woods, so we hurriedly put our shoes on, used their outside toilet, and said good-bye.

Rushing single file, we were about halfway across the field when we heard distant thunder and saw the tall weeds along our trail swaying in a fresh breeze. We laughed and shouted as large raindrops danced on us and the parched ground. But as the rumble of thunder became loud cracks of lightning followed by a sudden downpour, we began running like wild animals. We knew the danger of storms in open fields such as the pasture as well as under trees. The narrow path was muddy and slippery; that forced us to walk beside it in the wet weeds. As lightning intermittently brightened the darkened woods, I dreaded entering the spooky, dark shack.

We were all drenched by the time the thunder ceased and the rain let up. As we neared the shack, patches of sun showed behind the clouds. Then a most gorgeous, heavenly rainbow spread like a huge, colorful crown over our relatives' former home. Although the storm had turned part of our trip into a challenge, we were safe with the gift of a rainbow and were so grateful.

Our father once told us a story about rainbows. It was another hot day, and our porch had become shelter for those caught in the yard during a brief, sudden shower. The rain swayed with a breeze across the pasture; there were no cows in the vast, barbed-wired space, and no crop was planted. Mo, though, had said there had been wheat when I was too young to remember. I watched the rain beat down on the dry, red-clay hopscotch section of our yard. It made temporary dusty spots and forced old fallen chinaberries into the grassy edge. The smell of fresh, wet dirt filled the cooling air. Then the sun came out, and a beautiful rainbow appeared over the pasture. "It's been said if you throw a rock and hit the rainbow, you'll receive a pot of gold," Daddy said.

His serious tone prompted most of us children to begin collecting rocks in the yard and pasture and putting them in pockets and folding them in the front tails of our polo shirts. As free as birds, we spread out racing across the yard and pasture. We threw various sized rocks as hard as we could toward the rainbow. To our dismay, no one hit it. When we had worn ourselves out, we returned to the house panting like dogs. Mo stood in the doorway smiling as Daddy laughed hysterically. A pack of rich-smelling Camel cigarettes showed through his white, short-sleeved shirt pocket. We'd fallen for his prank. Nevertheless, we learned we could simply enjoy the rainbow's beauty without ever expecting to get more from it.

One Monday, Daddy's day off, he took a different route coming home. He didn't park in his usual spot at the bottom of the hill by the Jacksons, nor did he drive on the red-clay roadway between the pastures. Instead, he surprised us. Opening Mr. Shoemakers' gate, he took off flying across the empty pasture in his black '52 Ford, a trail of dust following. As we watched from our porch and yard, he raced toward his audience. Daddy's reckless driving excited us; with all that space, we saw no danger. His speeding car leaned to one side on two wheels and curved to suddenly stop parallel to our house as he prepared to leave the pasture. Soon, Rich and some of us were yelling out requests.

"Get a wheel, Daddy! Let me see you get a wheel!"

When we later teased him about his daring show, Daddy calmly said, "It's a Ford" and laughed aloud, knowing he had pleased us.

We all enjoyed spending time with Daddy in the summer when school was out especially on his day off. We were used to his impatience and his form of discipline—his belt instead of a hickory switch. For all of us, it was great to see him laugh.

One pleasant, dry day, Daddy offered to teach Mo to drive the family car. Even though she knew how impatient he could be, he convinced her it would be easy. She was willing to give it a try. Daddy backed the car toward our house and sat waiting in the big, empty pasture. Reluctantly, Mo got in. Daddy taught her the basics, but just as she feared, he became impatient as the car inched slowly forward. He demanded she step on the gas before she was ready. He assured her there was nothing she could hit but the barbed-wire fence and the gate, neither of which was nearby. As we children watched near the pasture's edge, that car suddenly took off. Like a race car driver doing stunts, Mo zigzagged across the pasture and came to a bucking stop just before smashing through Mr. Shoemaker's gate. Her show was just as exciting as Daddy's had been, but for him, that was the end of it. He drove back to park the car by our pasture's edge, and while he looked flustered, Mo got out smiling.

My mother was so excited because she'd no longer have to catch the city bus to town or Gastonia. Those days, after paying her fare, she'd have to walk down the aisle often passing just a few white passengers and lots of empty seats to find hers in the back. That was the African American section, and the last seat was particularly hot during summer.

The following Monday, Daddy took Mo driving again but on the smooth surface of Acme Road. In his mind, the road provided a more confined space with well-defined edges and light traffic. But Daddy's impatience and Mo's zigzag driving frightened both of them so badly that they gave up. Throughout the day, Mo talked to us about her unpleasant experience.

"Nat's so mean! He's not patient enough to teach anybody to do nothing! I just can't start out driving and rushing like him!" She paused thinking through his reaction. "He scared me half to death on that road, and, and I saw that car that was coming!" Mo said she was so "outdone" and vowed to never take another driving lesson from Daddy again. And she didn't.

On some Sunday afternoons, Daddy had money scrambles on our porch. After collecting lots of change at the barbershop, he'd throw up handfuls of coins from his pockets. All of us children would suddenly be on our knees laughing, screaming, and grabbing quarters, nickels, dimes, pennies, and a few fifty-cent pieces. We could spend whatever we managed to pick up on candy, such as a long-lasting Sugar Daddy or Goobers. Enjoying the extra money, we'd say, "Daddy, let's have another money scramble!"

One time, he came home a little tipsy and began passing out bills from his wallet. We felt rich; we were already planning on buying more than candy. Imagine our disappointment the next morning when Mo told us we had to return some of the money. After sobering up during the night, Daddy had realized he'd handed out more than $1 bills. We reluctantly gave up the bigger bucks.

There were other treats from Daddy in the summer. It was usually a Monday evening when one of us would spot him coming up the hill with a large watermelon bought off the produce truck. (He'd lined up a stash in the barbershop.) "Daddy's got a watermelon! Daddy's got a watermelon!" someone would shout, and several of us would run down the hill to meet him. On the large, flat rock in our yard across from the front window, Daddy cut long wedges for us with the butcher knife. Sweet, sticky juice ran down our naked bellies while yellow jackets swarmed around. Mo often had to remind us not to eat too much late in the evening because we might wet the bed.

Sometimes, an extra watermelon went into the branch to cool for another day. Daddy brought cantaloupes home too, which I began to dislike. Unlike the sweet watermelon, they were eaten in the kitchen as part of supper usually when we had fresh-stewed corn. To me, they smelled like the worn oilcloth on our table.

During the summer, Daddy took Cassie and me to spend time with Aunt Lydia sometimes even overnight. While Aunt Lydia slept on her back in her high cherry bed, Cassie and I shared a rollaway bed next to her. But they both fell asleep too soon. With only the sound of an ornate cherry clock ticking in the dark on the mantel, I laid there scared to death.

I remembered Uncle Clyde, who'd recently died. I imagined him in the casket in the next room and looked forward to daylight. Though the morning brought bright sunshine, a pale-green palm branch painted on Aunt Lydia's screen door would always remind me of the scary wake that had taken place there.

Aunt Lydia kept Cassie and me busy sweeping her front wooden porch. Then we swept clippings she'd trimmed from her low-growing hedges surrounding her small front yard. Out back, she had an old tree bearing freckled peaches like we used to have, and we ate freely.

For an indoor snack, we had watermelon sandwiches that consisted of a buttered biscuit with slices of the fruit. Or we'd have grape jam on refrigerated white bread, which I enjoyed. The cold sliced bread was better than a cold biscuit. At home, I preferred to place one in the hot oven to heat until the outside was crunchy.

As an older brother, Rich was invaluable to me. I can only imagine how bored life in our isolated area would've been without him. Along with Cassie, we'd shared many interesting experiences. Rich had numerous family responsibilities. On Saturday mornings in hot weather, he waited for the iceman at the top of the hill. When we heard the clanking bell from our house, he'd race to meet him for a 50¢ block of ice for our icebox. The twine around it served as a handle. The melting ice, though, sometimes rubbed against his dry, brown legs. He struggled on the downhill path, rested, then continued uphill to home.

Throughout the year, it was Rich's job to take the grocery list to the store on Saturday mornings. One day, he learned the white Radcliff family in the corner house was moving. Their furniture and other housing items were loaded on a pickup truck while the youngest Radcliff girl and boy played nearby. My siblings and I were saddened, but we hoped another family with lots of children would move in. To our disappointment, though, the new family was entirely different. There were no children, only Miss Bentley, who worked at the mill, and her elderly mother.

When Mo was returning from town one afternoon, Miss Bentley offered her a small Saturday-morning ironing job in her mill home. Mo had stopped working at the police officer's house, but he had recommended her to Miss Bentley. Because the job would be much closer to home, Mo accepted, again leaving Millie and Gwen in charge of us. We were generally cooperative.

Having a creative, mischievous mind, Rich often found ways to amuse himself and sometimes others. Miss Graham, the new white mill tenant's elderly mother, had a habit of sitting in her cushioned rocking chair on their front porch. On pleasant, sunny mornings, she'd stare across the street toward the distant Acme Mill. Returning from the grocery store, Rich decided to tease her by ducking by some short shrubs beside her house. When Miss Graham got up to search for him, holding his laughter, he'd duck just in time. But when she finally went inside and brought back her daughter, Rich ran as fast as lightning down the hill to home.

He couldn't stop laughing when he told us the story. We laughed too, but we knew Mo shouldn't hear that one. Most of us had already learned how to screen Rich's mischief. Imagine those women discovering a little African American boy, Maggie's boy, playing tricks on them.

Rich would take Mo's list to McAlbe's Grocers for later delivery and would often carry home an additional bag of groceries. Cassie and I sometimes made several trips to the store during the week for a few necessities. Occasionally, particularly heavy loads were separated and put in two large brown paper bags for us to carry home. Once, we were caught in a thunderstorm with a heavy downpour and our soaked bags burst. Running barefoot along the path, canned goods and other groceries rolling down the grassy hills by Acme Mill, we raced home empty-handed. Once the storm was over, we went back out and retrieved the groceries.

Before we ever left the house, Mo made sure our hair was combed and our clothes were clean and decent. She didn't want her girls or Rich to look like little "throwed-away children." Gwen had to comb my hair because Mo said I couldn't be still long enough for her to make straight parts and plait it. Having kinky hair and tender headed, I thought Mo didn't understand because her hair was soft and combed easily. I preferred my hair with a part down the middle with two plaits joined together on each side. However, I often had the popular three plaits or extra side ones.

Eventually, Gwen taught me how to plait hair, and Cassie and I practiced using Mr. Frazier's soda bottles. We had mostly Kool-Aid at home, mostly grape and cherry. Sometimes, fresh squeezed lemon was added, or we had fresh lemonade—six lemons on the list—but never sodas. For hair, Cassie and I filled the top of an open soda bottle with long, cut twine from Saturday's ice and secured it with a stick. We then combed the twine out, separated it into three parts, and plait it. Our fingers secured the strands as we alternated one over another. The bottle became a puppet we pretended to converse with. Wild onion patches on the back grassy slope were plaited too, the smell lingering on our hands for hours.

My sister and I had lots of fun playing together and even creating imaginary friends. I named mine Patty Ann, after me, while Cassie named hers Martha Ann. We talked about things we did with our friends. I enjoyed Cassie's sometimes puzzled expression when I made my stories sound so real. And Cassie got so good at her own pretense that I almost believed her. Neither of us ever admitted our fun was make-believe.

Just as my siblings and I learned we couldn't hit a rainbow, we learned we couldn't catch a bird by putting salt on its tail. One time, perhaps Rich wished he'd tried salt instead of a rock or even an old, dried chinaberry in his slingshot. After all, they were plentiful, readily available from our yard, and fit perfectly in his slingshot's tongue. Rich's aim probably wasn't that good that he'd hit a bird; he just enjoy chasing a moving target.

When Cassie and I were roaming the woods with him, he searched for new slingshot prongs in dogwood trees not far from the pasture's gate. Keeping Cassie in sight, I ventured away from the trees to the sunny edge where I discovered a blackberry bush on the backside of a thick shrub. The briars were loaded with big, ripened berries that I immediately started picking and eating. We had no containers, but I knew Mo would be excited about the new blackberry patch.

Preoccupied, Rich was looking up in the trees and throwing rocks at whatever he saw move. Just as I bent down to pick another berry, my whole world turned blacker than the fruit. My head had been bombed. Well, it felt that way. Rich had slammed a huge rock into the nearby bush and hit me on my head. At first, I had no idea what had happened; I just knew I was about to die. I cried out, running toward home and screaming like a gorilla was chasing me.

"I thought you wuz a bird!" Rich shouted. "I was throwing that rock at a bird. Tricie, wait! I thought a bird moved in that bush! I didn't know you wuz in 'ere!"

Rich was terrified too, and I heard him calling after me. I let myself through the pasture gate, holding my head just above my right temple. I ran as fast as I could through the dusty pasture. Our house looked so small, so far away. I was running so hard and fast it felt like a bone was piercing the bottom of my ribs. Mo must've seen us coming because she met me on the porch, shouting, "Lord have mercy what happened?"

Crying out, my mouth wide open and my head tilted backward, I held my breath for several moments, horrifying Mo. She yelled for me to catch my breath. Seeing the frightened look on her face, I tried to explain. "I wuz picking blackberries and ..." I could barely talk between sobs. "... and Rich hit me with a rock."

"Rich!" Mo shouted as she tried to examine my bleeding head. "You know better than to be throwing rocks! It's real dangerous to get hit in the temple!"

Aside from putting someone's eye out, Mo's worst fear about throwing rocks was for one of us getting hit in the temple.

"But I didn't mean to hit Tricie." His sad, cocker-spaniel eyes watered. "I thought I wuz throwing at a bird." Rich was sincere and scared for me just as much as for himself.

Well, I didn't die. Mo cleaned the open wound and doused it with hydrogen peroxide. A huge knot had formed. She warned me of the danger of going to sleep right after a hard hit on the head. I drank lots of water and sat in the big chair for a long time before lying across the bed. I fell asleep without having supper, washing up, or even saying my prayers. Mo scolded Rich, but when no hickory switch was mentioned, he hoped she'd get amnesia.

As busy as Mo often was, she did sometimes lose track of a promised whipping. Nonetheless, we were amazed at how much she did remember. She believed children should respect and obey grown-ups particularly their parents. Also, she reminded us that according to the Bible, our days could be shortened if we didn't. There should especially be no talking back, what she called sassing. When all else failed and she could tolerate no more disobedience, she'd resort to a whipping as her ultimate form of punishment. We were just too hardheaded, she said.

I always admired Mo and thought she was the ideal example of a mother. She was very hard-working but always carried herself like a lady. She didn't smoke or dip snuff as the women in our small neighborhood did, and I never heard her use profanity or saw her drink alcoholic beverages. While I usually respected her by being cooperative and soft-spoken when she asked me to do something, there were times when my behavior and attitude were unacceptable. By the time I was nine, Mo had long since warned me I was old enough to be getting whippings rather than a light spanking with her hand. My day came soon enough.

It was a hot summer afternoon, and I was wearing a sleeveless cotton dress. I must've been sassing her because Mo gripped my upper arm with one hand and began striking me with a skinny switch from the hedge bush. My dress tail flopping, I screamed out. Some of my siblings looked on, but their faces became complete blurs as tears rolled down my cheeks. I knew they felt sorry for me as I did for them whenever they danced around in a circle crying.

"You gonna be a good girl!" Mo yelled at me, forcing me to agree. I knew better than to disagree. "You gonna do what I tell you to do!"

"Yes 'am! Yes 'am!" I promised, but even that didn't stop her.

"You gonna stop sassing!" she demanded, both of us still moving in circles.

"Yes 'am! Yes 'am!" I was dancing a jig as if trying to avoid tall weeds or a snake on my way to the toilet. My tears dropped like rain, but Mo didn't notice, so I decided to hold my breath like I had when Rich hit me with the rock. My head thrown back, eyes practically closed, I made my body surrender. I went lifeless. I gaped my mouth wide open without making a sound. Mo immediately dropped the switch and grabbed my shoulders staring into my face and shaking me desperately.

"Catch your breath, Tricie! You better catch your breath!"

I knew she was afraid I might "cank away." Mo used that expression whenever one of her babies cried hard after a fall and appeared to lose his breath or be dying. But I couldn't just stop the moment she panicked, so I continued a bit longer, which was about all the breath holding I could bear. I was released. It had worked.

I tried the same trick during my next whipping, but Mo just got angrier when she discovered my scheme. She wasn't buying it, and she warned me it wouldn't work the next time either. I wondered if Rich had told my secret because he looked guilty and usually was.

Anyway, I learned that Mo was a lot smarter than I was and that I had better respect her and stop sassing. It was disrespectful for any of us to sass our parents. Even complaining or grumbling under our breaths in response to a parent's request was considered sassing. No matter how softly we uttered our grumblings, it was likely to be heard and our facial expression seen. We were supposed to be respectful to other adults too.

Summer was not always fun. Sometimes, there were terrifying experiences. One time, we found Dan, a toddler at the time, foaming at the mouth. He had drunk kerosene he'd discovered in a small can by the heater. Frightened and with no working transportation at that time, Daddy grabbed him in his arms and ran all the way to Dr. Walters in downtown Belmont. Dan would be all right with a prescription. All was normal again. And so the summer of 1953 ended.

## Chapter 9

# SPEECHLESS AND CHRISTMAS—GRADE 4

My fourth-grade classroom was in one of the lower brick buildings next to the sweet shop. There, after lunch, we could buy treats like candy, popsicles, and some school supplies. It was adjacent to the other fourth-grade classroom as there were two classes for each elementary grade level. Instead of meeting a new teacher, I had Miss Cranford again. We no longer sang the good-morning-to-you song. For devotion, we sang "America" and said the Pledge of Allegiance to the flag. Daily, each student also recited a short Bible verse, and together, we'd say the Lord's Prayer. In addition to church, I was already saying it at home too.

When we met in the other fourth-grade teacher's classroom, under her leadership, I became president of the Brownies. She'd talked the group through simple voting procedures. But that patient teacher had to tell me every word to say if we ever were to start a meeting. When Cassie became a Brownie, she thought she learned a new health song to fix her hair. She sang, "Milk, milk, we all like milk. Milk'll make your hair fix. Milk'll make your hair fix." She drank milk, but her hair didn't change; it was not "fixed." Later, she realized she had substituted the words *hair fix* for *healthy*. Milk was supposed to make her healthy.

Starting as early as October, we'd discuss Christmas with great anticipation. Then, with the beauty of the fall leaves and Thanksgiving excitement gone, December's wintry chill disrobed Belmont of most of its color. During trips to the spring, the wintry, naked tree branches and scattered evergreens along the path revealed a different kind of art. Our statuesque chinaberry tree stood with clinging clusters of ripened, golden-tan berries. The clothes and linens hanging on our clothesline got as stiff as boards. On gloomy, frigid days, both houses had smoke streams coming from their chimneys.

To get us through to spring, the family needed warmth, a hot stove for cooking, and water. As for every winter, a new pile of coal was delivered in late fall. The truck came down the red-clay, seldom-used roadway between Mr. Shoemaker's and Miss Dexter's pastures. Passing the far side of our chinaberry tree, it went under our wire clothesline and cut across our front yard of wild winter grass to get to the far side of our house. There was kindling inside to start the fires in the heater and cook stove, but like the coal, the wood pile soon needed replenishing.

Sometimes, Rich helped Millie and Gwen carry in wood and fill buckets of coal for the night; we called that night work. As our chores shifted, I began helping Rich with wood and coal, the palms of our hands becoming messy and black.

By December, we had firm ideas for our Santa Claus lists and asked for the toys we hoped to receive after a year-long wait. When one of us was bored, he or she would come out with, "Let's talk about what we're gonna git for Christmas!"

Mo could hear us talking from about anywhere in the house and would let us know if we were thinking unreasonably. "If y'all don't be good, Santa Claus's not gon' bring you anything," she'd warn us. "Nothing but a big, fat hickory set'n in the corner."

We knew to be good. After each reminder, we were cooperative and respectful when she'd ask us to do something. That included tasks we normally frowned upon such as emptying the slop jar used during the night. (We didn't run to the toilet in the dark.)

Finally, when it was time to search for a Christmas tree, most of us followed Mo to the edge of the pasture and through the woods. Bundled up, we found a tall, narrow cedar that could fit in the limited space in our house. Mo cut the tree down with our ax, and we dragged it home.

The tree filled the room with wonderful redolence. We put it up in front of the back window and decorated it with round, colorful, metal bulbs and bell-shaped ornaments. Small bits of cotton representing snowflakes were stuck all over the tree with the largest portion covering the base. A gold, cardboard star Mo purchased at Joe Farrington's dry goods store went on top. As the Christmas excitement escalated, days seemed to go by slowly, and we frequently wanted to know how many more days we had to wait for it. When one of us would ask, "How many mo' days 'fore Christmas?" Rich or an older sibling might say, "Not tomorrow, not the next day, not the next day, but the next day."

During the evening on Christmas Eve, most of the children in my family walked through the woods and Belmont Abbey to O' Conner's Grove Church for a Christmas pageant that always included the manger scene. With Miss Cranford's guidance, church youths displayed their talents, and my memorized parts became increasingly longer as I aged. At the end, every child along with siblings who did not participate in the program or did not attend received a brown bag that contained fresh fruits, nuts, and small pieces of hard Christmas candy.

Rushing home through the woods, we shivered in the cold. Dusk quickly became darkness; the sky allowed stars to gradually peek through. The night was still with just the sounds of our footsteps rustling on the fallen leaves. Over the bare treetops, melodious chimes from Belmont Abbey rang out "Silent Night," "Joy to the World," and "It Came upon a Midnight Clear." The sounds were as crisp and clean as the frigid air. I was mesmerized by those tones that echoed the songs we had sung in church earlier all about Jesus's birth. Mo said that was what Christmas was all about, not just getting toys. It was as if heaven had opened up and miraculously created the magical sounds that floated over the woods to our small neighborhood and made Christmas real.

We finally reached the clearing by Mr. Frazier's toilet. Our hearts were warm, and the heater inside our home warmed our bodies up. The excitement over new toys had peaked, and that night, we each went about "setting for Santa Claus," what we called preparing a personal spot for our toys. We lined the well-used, wooden kitchen chairs up against the kitchen wall. The chairs' thick finishes showed layer upon layers of paint ending in white with red trim. A small slip of notebook paper or a piece of brown grocery bag had a name and the list of items we wanted Santa to bring and was placed on the seat of each chair. Since Christmas was special, Mo baked a pineapple layer cake, Santa's favorite, and a coconut layer cake especially for the family. Otherwise, she didn't like to bake cakes because she didn't trust our oven's temperature.

As soon as darkness fell, Rich, Cassie, and I made tents in the same small bed. We burrowed beneath the covers and chatted about what Santa would bring us. I listened attentively as Rich lay by the window explaining how Santa would come flying through the air. He pulled back the lace curtain and held up the blinds enough to peer out. Staring into darkness, we saw red lights gliding high in the sky that convinced us Santa was looking for our house. We were ecstatic, and after expressing all our thoughts including what we'd play with first and what we'd share, we had difficulty settling down. Finally, we fell asleep on that longest night of the year.

The next day came. All of us were excited when we entered the kitchen to see our gifts. A variety of brand-new toys, clothes, and fruit had been placed on and in front of each chair according to the lists. The pineapple cake had been cut, and beside it, a bit of black coffee was left in a white, chipped cup. The room was so cold that the icing on the cakes had frozen. It was an exciting day as Cassie and I played with dolls and other toys while eating fruit and candy. Indeed, Christmas morning was a magical time. We soon became as tired as our parents, who'd slept late.

While I'd enjoyed being at home during Christmas, I'd missed the school activities and daily routines as well as my classmates. Some of them I considered my friends, and it seemed by now they and others could predict my behavior. I was still timid at school, and if a staring classmate said, "She's about to cry. Patricia is about to cry," my tears would start falling as others looked on. I'd been labeled, programed to perform accordingly. No one expected a positive change.

Our shortcut to the spring took us directly by Mr. Frazier's kitchen window. After all this time, Mo realized he and Miss Delphine might prefer a little privacy especially with the windows open during the summer. Come to think of it, she didn't like the idea that any visitor could suddenly come upon our exposed kitchen either. "Other people don't have their kitchens on the front," she told us and then Daddy when he came home from work. Again, he agreed.

Not long after the smokehouse was removed, the kitchen and back bedroom were switched. One Monday, Daddy and one of his friendly customers moved our heavy kitchen furnishings through the main room to the back bedroom. Millie and Gwen helped Mo with the kitchen chairs. My parents' small iron bed was moved to the main room for some of us children. Daddy bought a new rollaway bed that was stored behind the new kitchen door during the day. Each night, Mo prepared it for herself and Daddy. At first, the house was a mess with big pieces of furniture in small spaces. But eventually, all was put in place, and the house had a fresh, new look.

The new front room, our former kitchen, felt spacious with the red sofa bed, which was pulled out for the boys at night. At one end stood a small cigarette stand with a large amber ashtray, a cherished gift Mo had received from one of her brothers. The wardrobe, chairs, and a small oil heater that warmed the new space completed the room. At bedtime, the boys had to get there from our porch, which was a problem in cold weather. After drowsing by the heater in the main room with the family, the cold air was unwelcome.

After the new kitchen was all set up, a globe was bought for our kerosene lamp. For a long time, we'd had just one lamp and a flambo, which is what we called a lamp without a globe. The wick and flame were exposed after the globe was broken. Periodically, the smoke-stained glass needed cleaning, and moving it from room to room created opportunities for breakage. If Mo needed light in one of the other rooms, she'd say, "Excuse the lamp please" while the rest of us waited motionless in the dark for the lamp to return.

I had witnessed several classmates, usually boys, cry with embarrassment when Miss Cranford paddled their hands with her unbreakable wooden ruler when they broke class rules or were mischievous. (I'd seen Rich cry at home, but that was probably because he'd been punished for something.) When the boys were caught for something, they were frightened and humble during their punishment. Miss Cranford let them know who was in charge and that they needed to follow her rules or there would be more licks with her ruler. Those boys were just as human as I was; they expressed their uncontainable emotions.

Except for a new, big-city girl we considered fast because she had been exposed to too much for her young age, girls weren't often paddled. But the day she shared inappropriate pictures in the restroom, two girls got the stinging ruler as others who had looked at the pictures sat nervously in their seats. They were relieved when Miss Cranford calmed down and resumed her lesson. I felt proud she never had to paddle me; I was a good girl though I still found cause to cry. For example, even if someone said I had his or her pencil and I couldn't prove I didn't, to avoid further confrontation, I'd probably cry rather than defend myself. Or if someone talked mean to me, my feelings were hurt, and of course I'd cry.

One day, my group was reading "Rumpelstiltskin," the longest story in our reader. One of the girls read fluently; we listened to the rhythmic sounds of her voice as we followed along in our books. Though I was in the top reading group, it was impossible for me to match her or even the poorest reader because I had laryngitis; I could barely utter a sound before school, but I hadn't wanted to miss a day. When Miss Cranford called on me, I didn't know how to respond.

"Patricia, read." Our eyes met, but I said nothing. She tried again, her voice stern as she and others in the reading group waited. "Patricia, I said read!"

I glanced down at the reader, wondering if I could squeeze out a word. When I tried to begin however, I couldn't make a sound.

"You aren't going to read? You aren't going to read? Come here, Patricia!"

She was as furious with me as she had been with the girls and the unacceptable pictures. She sprang from her chair and slammed her book down. She was waiting for me in the corner of the room where her desk sat by the window. I was more frustrated than she was and began crying as I slowly walked down the aisle. My classmates had never seen me paddled during the three previous years. And of course the few whippings I'd gotten at home were unknown to them.

By the time I reached Miss Cranford's desk, she had the ruler ready in one hand while her other hand rested impatiently on her hip. I was petrified and embarrassed as the class watched.

"Hold your hand out, Patricia!"

I wiped the before-the-pain tears from my cheeks and slowly held out my right hand.

Without hesitation, I received ten stinging licks—a number ten on the pain chart. Miss Cranford didn't miss a beat. "You'll know the next time I call on you to read that you better read!" After she stored her ruler in the desk and started back to her big chair, she muttered under her breath, "Being so stubborn!" Disgusted, she motioned for me to return to my seat.

Miss Cranford had already labeled me stubborn in first grade when I was too shy to express myself. I sucked my lip and fondled my neck at home and had been labeled a crybaby at school.

I had seen some of my classmates discreetly pass notes across the aisle or in the back of the classroom, and they hadn't been caught, but I never thought to write one simple message to Miss Cranford with three little words: "I can't talk." For a while, she became the meanest teacher in the world. I didn't even want her to be my cousin anymore, but I kept that to myself.

In the spring of '54, like every year, purple and white flowers adorned our chinaberry tree while some golden-tan berries still hung in clusters from the winter. When the flowers became green chinaberries, Cassie and I picked them to string with needle and thread to make bracelets and necklaces. Too soon, our lovely, live jewelry shriveled and made our hands stink and taste bitter.

Knowing we wanted something girlie and fun to do, Mo taught us how to make small, even running stitches and showed us how to use a brown paper pattern and fold pieces of an old, clean, white sheet to make little ragdolls stuffed with cotton. Perfecting our skills, we made several dolls of various sizes and stitched on faces and twine hair that made them look like little white gingerbread people. Sewing would hold our interest for a while at least until something new struck our fancy.

Mr. Shoemaker planted wheat in the pasture that spring, and the vast area had begun changing from a barren field to a light shadowing of tender new plants that soon became a blanket of vibrant green wheat. The color was as beautiful as life and hope, new beginnings. We weren't to tread across the pasture, but what harm were a few light footsteps occasionally? A straight line from our front door across the pasture led to our familiar section of woods, but Mr. Shoemaker probably wouldn't agree with our notions.

Change was good, and like the pasture, our family was changing. While there were already four girls and three boys, Mo was expecting her eighth child.

# Chapter 10

## THE DENTIST AND TRASH

On Saturdays, Mo sometimes took Cassie and me to catch the city bus to downtown Gastonia. She'd shop there for special items such as Easter hats or sewing supplies. Sometimes, we needed other items that weren't available at our drugstore and we'd go to the one farther away. On one hot day, Mo wore her hair rolled across the back of her neck secured with bobby pins. From the main shopping building that housed our grocery store, we took a shortcut down a cool, wooded, wide path that led to an alternate bus stop for our Gastonia trip.

Adjacent to that drugstore was a huge, redbrick church that always aroused my curiosity. Though not labeled for whites only, we knew it was. The church was in a white area, and no African American church in Belmont was as large and stately as that one. Except for the white Radcliff girls, who showed some similarities to my family, whites seemed so different; we didn't even think alike. In our small, plain church, Sunday school lessons were about Jesus; we sang about Him and heard preaching from the Bible. Did white folks have the same or similar church services? It was as if there were a big secret I wanted to expose. If only I could discreetly peek inside on a Sunday, look around, and listen, I might understand the impervious white world surrounding us. That was I knew impossible.

When the bus came, we found our seats in the back.

Occasionally for a special treat, Mo made sweet bread—not sweet enough to be a cake but too sweet to be called bread. It filled our chipped porcelain baking pan, and we enjoyed it as a dessert or snack. One day, Mo placed a pan of freshly baked sugar cookies high on top of our kitchen cabinet to cool and remain hidden for later. Rich saw her, and as soon as she left the room, he climbed on a chair and took a few. When he climbed down, Cassie was standing there staring at him. Rich pleaded for her not to tell and gave her a cookie. But as soon as they saw Mo coming through the kitchen doorway, Cassie said, "Mo, Rich didn't eat any o' those cookies."

Mo scolded Rich for eating the cookies he knew were for after supper. Rich learned he couldn't trust Cassie to keep a secret.

When Rich wasn't traipsing through the woods with his slingshot and one or two white boys from the mill village, Cassie and I enjoyed following him. We trusted his leadership. Climbing trees, swinging on sturdy limbs that branched parallel to the ground, and placing both feet between his hands to flip backward and land flatfooted on the ground were among his favorite challenges. We called that "skinning the cat."

"Tricie, I bet you can't do this!" he'd say.

After that, sometimes, when we saw Rich climb a tree or skin the cat, Cassie and I often tried it too. When Mo cleared a section of thicket and small trees by the pasture's edge on the far side of our house, like any change, the new space was exciting. We skinned the cat on a now-exposed sturdy tree. Soon, Cassie and I'd make playhouses in the flat, shady clearing.

Sometimes, we took pots on our adventures and returned home with enough blackberries for Mo to make a cobbler. One time, Rich got us lost, and we wandered around in several unfamiliar areas that seemed subtly different. We became anxious as it grew late, and it took us a long time to finally reach the edge of Mr. Shoemaker's pasture. At the gate, we saw our house in the distance. But before we got too happy, Rich said, "Y'all know you can't tell Mo. If y'all tell, you know she won't let y'all come with me no mo'."

As children, we weren't allowed to use the word *lie*. Instead, we said someone or another was "telling a story." That time, Rich wasn't sure he could trust Cassie because she'd recently told Mo about the hidden cookies.

"We not gon' tell," we said when he pressed us.

That was always our promise, and it relieved Rich though sometimes just temporarily.

Early that summer, some of Reid High's students became eligible for treatment at a dental clinic held in the brick homemaking building across a sidewalk from my fourth-grade class. Millie, sixteen, needed dental work, and just for company, I rode with her on the big city bus. When we arrived, we sat in wooden student chairs along the back wall. The dentist stood at his big chair in the middle of the multipurpose room. There was no line for treatment; it was just the dentist and us. He called out, "Mildred Littleton" and gestured for her to sit in his chair. I waited patiently watching the dentist in his white jacket work in Millie's mouth. He talked to her in a gentle, sweet voice.

"Open, open wide. This won't take long. Open wide, please."

Without warning, he yanked a tooth from the back of Millie's mouth causing her to let out a quivering grunt of pain. I was glad I hadn't been in that chair. Teary eyed, she waited until he was done and went to the restroom in the front corner of the room leaving me alone with the dentist.

He gestured to me. "Next. Come. You're next."

I didn't move. I stared at him. When I realized he was serious, I said, "No sir. I just came to keep my sister company."

The dentist ignored that and gestured again.

Hypnotically, I strolled across the floor and sat in his big chair. He said, "Open wide please. This won't take long."

Before I knew it, that man had pulled two of my back teeth! Feeling tricked, I cried all the way home.

Millie was easygoing and cooperative; she did a lot of work around the house. She sometimes straightened, dusted, and swept most of the three small rooms. As she worked, she sang songs she'd learned in glee club or relating to her beginning to like boys. If one of us was singing a song, she'd sing that too. Gwen on the other hand refused to hold her tongue, and Mo could detect the faintest mumble under her breath. That was sassing. Most of the time, the conflict was over a grits or oatmeal pot or something else she hadn't washed well. She sometimes wanted to leave pots soaking but couldn't because Mo needed them for cooking our next meal. She sulked whenever she had to rewash any pot. Also, unlike Millie, Gwen preferred dancing and listening to music rather than singing, washing dishes, or cleaning the kitchen. She did well helping elsewhere though. She didn't mind helping Mo cook, wash clothes, or comb and straighten hair.

Out front, Mr. Shoemaker's tall wheat that swayed in the breeze had turned a golden tan similar to the chinaberries in late fall and winter. But another feature outside Miss Dexter's pasture held our interest. An enormous garbage dump was in a clearing in the woods. On quiet days, we could hear the loud sounds of a new load of trash being delivered. Later, we made our way to examine what had arrived. Rich, Cassie and I and sometimes Carl found the trash piles fascinating. They held things that were very different from what we had in our trash. We searched for toys and other things. The trash gave us insight into what white society was like. I concluded that white folks, probably mill workers since they lived in our area, dipped a lot of snuff and must've had a lot of aching backs. That I'd surmised due to the number of snuff and Doan's pills metal containers we discovered.

Sometimes, we found good toys and wondered why they'd been thrown away. We'd take them home and clean them up. If when digging with long sticks on top of the trash pile we found a doll with an arm or leg missing, we'd search diligently until we found the missing limb. Often, our discoveries were so fascinating that we'd forget all about the time. Other times, we found only junk we'd throw back into the nasty pile with broken glass and countless other sharp objects.

Cassie and I found things for our playhouses, even perfect dishes. Though they were free of chips and cracks, they never ended up in our kitchen. Mo said they'd never be clean enough to use, and neither did she like us bringing home a lot of junk. Nevertheless, Cassie and I enjoyed collecting odd-shaped items or containers including the elongated Doan's tins that were special to us. For headaches, Mo took only Bayer aspirin or Goody's Powder. Exhausted after bending over to wash loads of clothes, she had to sit down a short while or rest her aching back in bed at night. She'd say she was "give out."

One hot summer day, an African American woman, Bertha, driving an old pickup half filled with junk, came to our area. She was collecting metal and offered us money for what we found. We searched the outskirts of our familiar property and brought back pieces of metal of various sizes. Much of it came from the trash piles. I earned a lot of money that day—50¢. Those exploring and trash-collecting days satisfied us until other interests occurred in our neighborhood or somewhere in the woods.

## Chapter 11

# NEW NEIGHBORS AND A REAL TRICK

During the early summer of '54, changes occurred in our small area of two houses. Mr. Frazier and Miss Delphine moved out, and the place was dark and spooky for the short time the house was vacant. When we passed it at dusk to go to the spring, Rich and I were sure we saw a ghost, which we called a haint, on the porch.

Finally, a woman named Hazel Simpson moved in with her three children—Phyllis, who was about my age, Barbara, who was younger, and Stevie, their youngest, a boy. I watched from our tire swing as they went in and out from their front porch. Hazel was a large woman who was dark complected. She was taller, heavier, and much younger than Mo. Her straightened hair was thick, almost shoulder length, and curled under slightly.

We felt good about having new neighbors especially other children with whom we could play. And though Mo and Miss Delphine had been friendly, it was nice for Mo to again have adult interaction sometimes during the day. The families borrowed from each other; Hazel occasionally needed a cup of sugar or an egg or two, or we used her straightening comb, which was of better quality than ours. Rich borrowed Hazel's grass cutter that was more efficient than our grass slinger, which worked best on tall weeds.

Neither Hazel nor Mo had a television to enjoy the soap operas or "stories." They instead listened to battery radios; the sleepy organ music became dramatic at times. The Jacksons and Miss Emma, our neighbors at the bottom of the hill, had TVs. During the week on summer afternoons, we could hear Miss Emma's TV blaring through her screen door because her front room was close to our path. The people on TV always sounded like serious adults with problems they just couldn't resolve. I knew those programs had nothing to do with me or any children since none was talking and nothing that was said sounded like fun.

Mo took on an additional light ironing job working once a week for Miss Dawson. She didn't live in the mill village but in a two-story brick house near the Stowe Spinning area. One evening, I went with Mo to work and watched her iron on the second floor. Another time, Miss Dawson gave her several *McCall's* magazines with paper cutout dolls inside. I had fun dressing them by folding back the attached paper flaps on their cutout clothes.

Hazel shared her *True Confessions* and *Romance* magazines with Mo. They were very different, though; they had hardly any pictures. But the stories inside filled a void for both women. They offered something they could discuss in casual meetings between the yards. Mo didn't have much time for reading, but when she discovered in one of Hazel's magazines an advertisement for a hair product, she got excited. It was called Straight & Silky and was guaranteed to straighten hair. Mo ordered a jar; she wanted a change from her natural curls. A short time later, the company had her money and Mo still had her curls. She pleaded with Daddy to cut her hair since he cut other women's hair in attractive styles. Preferring her hair long, he refused; he told her to leave it alone. Mo soon became less interested in romance stories and special hair products.

One morning when the air was cool, Cassie, Rich, and I made several trips to the spring to fill the large tin tubs for the family's wash. Millie and Gwen helped Mo scrub clothes on the washboard and boil the whites in our black, sooty wash pot that sat over a fire.

Mo's hair, which was in two thick, long, loose, casual plaits in the back, wasn't fastened by bobby pins at the base of her neck. Using a long broomstick, she lifted hot items from the pot to the tub of rinse water. At night during the summer, she reminded us that our white sheets were hard to scrub clean so we were never to fall asleep with dirty feet from going barefoot all day.

More water was needed to rinse the white and dark clothes before wringing them out and hanging them on the clothesline. Propped up with two poles placed far apart, the wire line extended from one of the chinaberry tree branches across the grass in our front yard to one of Mr. Shoemaker's fence posts. If necessary, small articles of clothing were sometimes spread over wild shrubs by his pasture.

Most of the time, Mo washed clothes on the far side of our house. Sometimes, she washed a small load on our porch. One day, Hazel suggested a way we might shorten our numerous trips to the spring on washday. The weather was pleasant when we propped our two washtubs—one for washing and the other for rinsing—on old wooden chairs under the shade of Hazel's apple tree. They were chatting, laughing, and scrubbing. Then Mo screamed. A long green snake had fallen from the tree into her sudsy water. She dumped the tub, and all of us children rushed to watch the slithering snake. Hazel hit it with her hoe to capture it and slung it to the edge of the woods near her toilet. Then she and Mo continued with their wash laughing and talking as if they were the same age with much in common. The excitement died down. Cassie and I played with Phyllis and Barbara on that one day Mo washed clothes in Hazel's yard.

In summer sometimes, the blistering, North Carolina heat was barely tolerable; hardly a breeze would stir. Even with the main door wide open and the few windows propped up with chopped-off broomsticks, it was too hot for all seven of us children to remain inside. The only way to escape the heat was to sit on the edge of our porch with legs dangling from the slightly high end or to rest and play under the shade of our towering chinaberry tree.

When the sun hid behind the clouds, Rich cut our grass, the long blades forming a thin bed over the yard. His work wasn't complete though until he coaxed Carl in short pants and no shirt to roll in the cool grass. It was a trick of course. Rich knew Carl's damp back would soon be itching and he'd be unable to reach it to scratch.

In addition to mowing, Rich was responsible for refilling our water buckets for the night. After Cassie and I finished washing the supper dishes, the cooler temperature and warm evening breeze beckoned us outside. Rich lingered with us happy to absorb that peace. Dusk rapidly became darkness. Mille and Gwen helped Mo carry in a sheet loaded with white clothes she'd removed from the clothesline. In passing, Mo would casually remind Rich he had to "get up" the night water. She warned him he shouldn't let it get too late before going to the spring.

"I'm not gonna forget, Mo," Rich would say. But he'd continued chiseling his slingshot prong.

She came back. "Rich, you *better* get to that spring and get up that night water right now! I've done told you! There'll be none to cook with in the morning!"

Busy admiring his slingshot prong, smooth and looking good, Rich completely forgot about going to the spring. Afraid to go alone in the dark, he pleaded with Cassie and me to go with him. However, none of us relished being in those woods at night not even together. Along with the possibility of unseen snakes on the path, we had heard too many ghost stories.

Consequently, in his brown cotton shorts and colorful striped polo, Rich gathered the two water buckets and rushed off to the spring. Mo, my sisters, and I watched from the safety of our porch as Rich passed Hazel's apple tree. He continued down the path toward her toilet, the usual resting spot for both families, and disappeared into the woods. No full moon lit the route that night. I felt sorry for Rich. I'd been too afraid to help him.

Meanwhile, Mo grabbed a fresh white sheet from the big chair where she had placed the bundle of clothes and linens. We giggled as she rushed through Hazel's yard that was dimly lit by a glimmer of light from their main room. The family was oblivious to anything transpiring outside. Mo stood by the path beside Hazel's toilet. Laughing softly in the dark, she placed the sheet over her entire body while standing as still as a statue. We stood at the edge of Hazel's yard smiling in anticipation. Soon, Mo heard Rich coming up the path panting. As he rushed through the woods, water splashed on his bare, ashy legs. When he neared the toilet where he would rest, Mo's gentle move was all it took to get his attention. "*Owwww! Owwww!*" he suddenly screamed, more water splashing from his buckets as he started running.

Mo followed him in the dark calling his name, "*Rich! Rich!*" She laughed as she stumbled over the sheet as she removed her disguise. She called for him to stop running. She knew she had to make him slow down so he'd stop spilling so much water—nobody was going back to the spring to refill the buckets that night.

Still yelling, "*Owwww!*" Rich set the buckets down by Hazel's steps and ran up on our porch where we all stood laughing. His mouth was wide open. He looked scared out of his mind. Never had I seen him as frightened as that night, not even when Daddy was about to take his belt off for a whipping.

All of us except Rich were still laughing when we entered the house. I wished I could have seen his eyes that were probably as big as bogie marbles when he saw Mo, the ghost. For a while, he wouldn't talk to anyone. He suspected we'd been in on the prank. Nevertheless, that was the last time he waited until after dusk to get night water.

Mo needed laughs too. Her sense of humor often came alive even when she was exhausted from washing all day. Occasionally, she found time to have fun with us. Sometimes during the summer, she played softball with us in the large grassy area of our yard near the pasture. The field was adorned with Queen Anne's lace, my favorite wildflower. But that year, though having help with household duties, she was a very busy and often tired pregnant woman. Nonetheless, she expressed her happiness and contentment with her children. That was wonderful.

## Chapter 12

# THE LAST CHILD—GRADE 5

From the café next door to the barbershop, Daddy sometimes brought us Lilly Dillies, a flavorful icy treat in small polka-dot paper cups. Once, we waited up late for him, but he forgot.

Another night when he remembered, we were very drowsy and sitting up and fighting sleep. The cold, melting delight woke some of us up for a while, but that could happen only during the summer.

Though we all had been excited when Hazel and her family moved in, she often caused Mo stress over minor issues. For example, if Cassie and I played checkers or jacks with her girls and Phyllis lost, she complained to her mother that we'd cheated. She'd order her girls to stay in their yard and play with each other. If we were in their yard, we always knew when it was time to go home.

At one point, there were more bad times than good times. Hazel and Mo still had adult conversation and depended on each other, but there were times when we just didn't understand Hazel's actions. Soon, our mothers' interactions like ours with her children became increasingly difficult. Hazel's behavior disturbed Mo, who was invariably blamed when Hazel or her children were dissatisfied. As an excuse to declare her displeasure, Hazel would return some borrowed item and pout like an unhappy child. Since we didn't know how to label such strange behavior, we'd say she was "acting funny."

Mo sometimes vented to us. "Hazel knew she didn't have to give that back," she'd say. "Chaps are gonna be chaps and act like that sometimes. Parents have to correct their own children." Mo thought Hazel was being childish, and we knew the situation was becoming too much for her to handle. We concluded Hazel was unhappy for some unknown reason; it was up to us to be more careful in dealing with her and her children.

Cassie, Rich, and I occasionally ran errands to the drug or grocery store for Hazel. One time, she needed several food items to tide them over until her check arrived. When asked, Rich agreed to go to the store. She handed him a $10 bill along with a list written in pencil on a piece of a brown paper bag. As usual, she said he could have a quarter for going.

When Rich returned from the store with the large bag of groceries, he lingered as Hazel placed a loaf of bread, several canned goods, sliced bologna wrapped in butcher paper, a quart of sweet milk, and grits on her kitchen table. Rich handed her a $5 bill with a few coins and the grocery list. After Hazel glanced over it, she thanked him for going and gave him the coins to add to his already-spent quarter. Rich left, the screen door slamming behind him.

Later that evening, Rich and I had chores to do at home including carrying water from the spring for washing. When we reached Hazel's, she emerged from her kitchen and called Rich inside. Before I headed home with my bucket of water, I heard Hazel question him about a missing $5 bill. I was concerned; her tone of voice sounded harsh, accusing. When I informed Mo, she immediately stuck her feet in her slides. Holding the bottom of her enlarged stomach, she rushed to Hazel's house as if she had been sent for. I followed and sat with Hazel's children on their porch.

"Who else would have taken the money?" Hazel asked after explaining about the missing $5.

"My chaps know better than to be stealing," Mo replied softly.

"But Rich was the only person in here and knew 'bout that money!"

Hazel roamed about the kitchen peering under the table and around her free-standing cabinet. Rich looked directly at Mo. Mo turned to him. "Do you know anything about this?" she asked anxious for an honest answer.

"Hazel gave me a quarter for going and I spent it at the sto'," he whispered. "Then she gave me the seventeen cents I gave back to her with the five-dollar bill. I don't know what she did with it."

Mo believed her son though she had carefully analyzed him through the years. She'd learned when he was lying or trying to worm his way out of a sticky situation. Mo nodded, but not wanting to get into a dispute with Hazel, she didn't respond.

Soon, Hazel's small kitchen was crowded with Gwen, Cassie, and me all searching for the money. We looked under the table and around the wood stove where half a pot of white stewed potatoes sat. Coming up empty, we searched around the cabinet and other unlikely places such as the windowsill through which a breeze flowed.

Assured that Rich hadn't taken the money, Mo looked as Hazel moved the icebox out from the wall. Leaning over and gazing behind it, Mo shouted, "There it is, on the floor!"

Hazel bent down to retrieve the bill. "*Oh! Oh!*" she yelled moaning in pain and grabbing her right eye. She had stuck it on a penny nail protruding from the faded white, wooden bead board wall. Mo rushed Rich to the Jacksons' to get someone to drive Hazel to the doctor. Holding her belly, she stooped to retrieve the wadded bill and handed it to Hazel. The rest of us cleared out for home. We declared Hazel shouldn't have accused Rich that way. She left for the doctor and returned a couple of hours later with a patch over her eye.

At first, Hazel couldn't accept that a breeze from the open window or that forever-slamming screen door was to blame. She offered no apology but eventually dropped the issue. Mo didn't need the aggravation, and Hazel had no interest in admitting she'd been wrong. Our relationship with the Simpsons was already fragile. At that point, another bit of Hazel's integrity peeled away.

About a month after my tenth birthday, Mo's health was in decline. She was in danger of going into premature labor two months too soon. Concerned, Daddy called us together. "I want you chaps to mind your mother. Maggie can't work like she's been. All y'all need to help out. If she tells you to do something, you do it." We stared into his eyes. His tone and words were serious. "Don't let me hear tell of y'all sassing your mother, you hear me?"

"Yes sir," we responded in sad monotones.

Daddy removed his straw hat from the top knob of a ladder-back chair. Mo lay in bed. He held it in place on his head while he bent down to give her a quick peck on her cheek.

From the window, we watched him go down the hill to his car. His short-sleeved, light-blue shirt exposed his sleeveless undershirt, a low scoop under his neck and armpits. It was Daddy's job to step in now and again. He made sure we respected Mo and helped her as much as we could. However, his firm tone had frightened us. We knew he meant business. We had to do what he and Mo asked the first time they asked.

I was old enough to realize Mo's life simply shouldn't be taken for granted. She could die. Sometimes when we were sassy and not minding her, she'd let us know one day she wouldn't be around. We'd have regrets. I couldn't imagine living without her; she knew everything a good mother needed to know. She took care of us when we were ill. Sometimes, we had high fevers, bad colds, measles, or chicken pox. She put a band of cooked onions or Vick's VapoRub on our chests. She treated all our frightening injuries in Daddy's absence. She was the perfect mother. I wanted to be just like her when I grew up.

Since Mo's health limited her usual activities, Aunt Thelma helped out by making dresses for Cassie and me. She was an excellent and frugal but creative seamstress. She knew how to use the scraps from our printed cloth for trim on her girls' dresses. That was quite surprising at first notice. Compared to ready-made, store-bought clothing, the cloth in our homemade dresses had unique designs not likely to be duplicated.

One fall Saturday, Shaggy waited with us on the slope in Miss Dexter's pasture. Rich scurried up the pine tree to shake the muscadine vines that grew there. The sweet, ripened fruit were like big, black marbles rolling downhill toward the branch. Several of us gathered all we could to eat and take home as always before the cows came to drink.

School had begun. I was in fifth grade. One Saturday when Mo was ready to deliver, Millie rushed to the Jacksons to have someone call for an ambulance. When it finally arrived, it broke down on the crosstie bridge. Daddy had to come home and rush Mo to the African American hospital in Gastonia. Otherwise, he would have met the ambulance there.

Knowing Daddy's usual speed, I couldn't imagine a faster yet safer ride.

Later that day, Daddy approached the yard with an enormous smile plastered on his face. "Cassie's not the baby girl anymore!"

I was elated that Andrea was the new baby girl who had replaced Cassie as the youngest. Any new baby brought excitement, but that time, I had new feelings. When we were very young, it had bothered me that because Cassie was the baby girl, Daddy would pick her up first, kiss her on the cheek, smile, and talked to her. I couldn't understand why he didn't pick me up first. (I'm sure he treated me the same when I was the baby girl, but I was too young to remember that.) I recall times when I waited watching as he turned to Cassie; I hoped he wouldn't forget me. While growing up, I considered Cassie and me as equals, but I felt Daddy favored her. And considering her young age, I'm sure she was oblivious to my feelings, but so was Daddy it seemed.

I adored and treasured all the girlie things Cassie and I did together. Of the four girls, we were just two years apart in age; she was the one close to me. The two of us had so much in common. My affection for her never wavered. Nevertheless, I couldn't express that extra satisfaction, these new feelings, to any family member.

Andrea was ten years younger than me. We had all been breast-fed, but when a baby in our family was old enough for the bottle but too young to hold it, several older children helped feed him or her and would sing to and rock crying babies to sleep almost going to sleep ourselves. And we changed lots of diapers.

Each child definitely made a difference in our house. We ranged in shades from very light brown to very dark, but not one was better than the others; dark was as precious as light. One of the most hurtful expressions Mo warned us against was calling any sibling "black." Though I don't recall experiencing it in Belmont, some whites were known to use *black* to demean African Americans, something we all would've despised.

Even with a new baby in the family, there was still time for fun. Mr. Shoemaker's wheat was inviting. We ran and played hide and seek in sections of the pasture near our house. Even more exciting was to run as far as the center toward the gate. We'd almost get lost and had to call out to each other. It was like running through a huge, never-ending maze. Unaware of our game until Mr. Shoemaker complained of large areas of flattened wheat, Mo made us stop. Shortly after the complaint, our rent was due. Rich, who often took the $6 to his house, hoped Daddy would take it that time. Luckily, the farmer wasn't at home. Rich gave the rent to his wife. Mr. Shoemaker was not unkind, but Rich didn't want to risk a fresh scolding.

Once school began, we saw very little of the Simpsons particularly during the cold winter months. The doors and windows of our houses were shut as tightly as possible. One very cold evening before supper, in the quietness of our warm, cozy room, some of us were doing homework. We heard a faint knock at our door. It was Phyllis shivering in an unbuttoned wool coat and holding an empty coffee cup. She glanced around the busy room unsure where to focus. She shyly directed her attention to Mo, who was standing in the kitchen doorway.

"Miss Maggie, Mama said could she borrow a cup of sugar? She said she pay you back when she git groceries Sadday."

"She sure can. Got plenty of sugar in there."

Mo was glad to be helpful knowing Hazel was probably in the middle of cooking just as she was. Hearing silverware clang during trips to the spring had told us our families ate supper about the same time. A cup of sugar was the least Mo could do; Hazel had been so kind after the baby. Of course, Mo would've still given the sugar even on one of Hazel's worst days.

"Tell Hazel she don't have to pay me back. I might need to borrow som'n from her one day."

Though Hazel had been in a good mood at the time, she was still temperamental. When she was upset with Mo usually over some silly conflict her children had had with Cassie and me, her friendly attitude shifted. She became negative and cold for several days or more. During that time, she returned everything she had borrowed from us—eggs, sugar, whatever—through one of her girls. It was as if she was deliberately being as difficult and contrary as she could to cause friction between our two families.

Sometimes, Mo was able to smooth the matter over and regain harmony, reminding Hazel how children occasionally behaved. Mo had had lots of practice. Other times, Mo just allowed Hazel to speak her mind while trying to avoid fueling her fire.

One day that fall, I came home from school to hear a loud noise as I approached the house. A white man was sitting on a tractor circling the pasture to harvest Mr. Shoemaker's wheat. A cloud of dust surrounded him, and rectangular bails of brownish yellow wheat were dropped all over. After playing in Mr. Shoemaker's wheat field, we had left plenty for him.

That year, I had my first male teacher, Mr. Harris. It took some time getting used to his strictness. His voice was heavy. His harsh tone made me anxious. I'd thought Miss Cranford was mean. Mr. Harris used a small leather strap resembling a beaver's tail whereas Miss Cranford had used a wooden ruler. He commanded students to place their feet side by side on two of the beige squares on the tiled floor. With a sly grin, he'd say teasingly, "Tune it over" instead of "Turn it over." When the student bent over and was facing the floor, he'd say, "Place your hands on your knees please."

One day, Mr. Harris left Clara in charge; she was the classmate who had snatched my love letter in third grade and later became my friend. He told her to take names of anyone who talked in his absence. After he left, the class was briefly quiet but then became unsettled. As several students were talking loudly, our teacher discreetly reentered the room. "I know this is not my class!" His frown was frightening. He retrieved his strap from his desk drawer.

Names for practically everyone in the class were on the list, including mine and most of the other girls. If we were caught whispering just one word, our names were added. After Mr. Harris told us to put our feet together on a square of floor tile and bend over, he was shameless. The sounds of the punishment from three firm licks across our hips filled the room as did our sniffles.

During that week while I was in the school cafeteria, I began to cough continuously. After eating vegetable soup for lunch, I felt a very thin, wire-like shaving from the rim of a can caught in my throat. Outside in a play area, I cried and continuously tried to clear my throat. Nearby, several boys shot marbles while girls jumped rope and played hopscotch. Mr. Harris said I'd be all right, and my classmates seemed to believe him.

At home, I finally coughed up the metal shaving. My silly thought was, *If only I had coughed the metal up at school and laid it on Mr. Harris's peanut-butter sandwich. Then he'd have known I hadn't cried for just anything but about that little thing.* I chuckled to myself. At least at home, my mother, concerned about my constant coughing, had believed me.

On another day, Mr. Harris remained in our classroom while the boys played baseball and the girls played softball. On cold, sunny days, we were protected by our wool coats and headscarves. Most of us wore black-and-white or brown-and-white oxfords and bobby socks. Teams were chosen, and one of the girls enjoyed taking the last hit for those who would otherwise strike out. She was the oldest and tallest in the class. One day, I hit my ball and raced to first base as my team cheered. Then I raced to second, unintentionally bumping into Sarah, who missed the ball thrown to put me out. I was safe, but she yelled, "Patricia, look what you did! You tore my coat! I'm gonna tell!"

"No I didn't!" I kept my foot on second base.

"You did too!"

She became physical. Without thinking, I did too. I saw her surprised facial expression; her hand suddenly covered her bottom lip. I was as scared as a snake facing a hoe. I headed across the field to the classroom, Sarah tromping behind me. I started crying. I knew I was in trouble.

Mr. Harris was stunned because he had never seen me as upset as I was that day. When he talked to us, I learned one of the boys in our class had pulled Sarah's coat collar earlier causing the rip. He made us apologize to each other for shoving and punching. I didn't want to be labeled a fighter though I had caused some noticeable damage to Sarah's bottom lip. I had defended myself but didn't want to be labeled an aggressive student who got in trouble. I desired to remain the rather quiet, easygoing, good student I was.

# Chapter 13

## SHAGGY, BUSINESSMEN, AND DOUGHNUTS

Hazel's neighborly attitude held that Easter. For the first time, we had an egg hunt at the edge of the woods across from her house instead of in our yard. The Simpson children participated. We all had fun playing in a different section of our surroundings while Shaggy roamed about with us.

My family had become as attached to Shaggy as we had been to Brownie before him. There were no more chickens to chase, just Rich and us to trail to the spring and nearby areas. Even though Brownie had died, we took for granted Shaggy would be with us for as long as we could imagine. But in time, Shaggy changed. One crisp, sunny morning in late spring, we noticed he wasn't his lively, tail-wagging self. He was drooling and restless; he was making weird growling sounds as he rolled in the tall grass by the fishpond. Mo said he had gone mad and warned us not to get close.

I don't know who sent for Mr. Ben Mathow, but he came up the hill in his police uniform, his gun attached at his hip as always. Mo had warned us to stay in the house, where we watched and listened through the open side window. The two conversed near the fishpond. I didn't understand why the policeman was there. It was too early for Kool-Aid, as he'd once had a drink at our house on a hot summer day. And Mo no longer ironed for his family. Why was he looking at our dog? Could he make Shaggy better?

Pulling back the lace curtains for a clearer view, we peered out the window. Mo was in her usual stance, shoulders back, arms folded against her stomach. Her cotton dress swayed in the morning breeze. Then she turned her back to the officer, her head down, and walked toward our porch. I saw Mr. Ben Mathow reach for his pistol and point it at Shaggy. Suddenly, a loud, piercing sound came from his gun. Our policeman and family friend had shot and killed our dog.

When Mo entered the house, we were all crying. She explained Shaggy had gotten rabies and could've made all of us sick. The officer had no choice. Rich dug a shallow grave near the outer edge of our yard by the pasture. He covered Shaggy with red clay and clumps of grass and placed yellow dandelion flowers on top. Several of us gathered around the grave. Rich, teary eyed, spoke a sorrowful good-bye: "Shaggy was a good dog. Followed me 'bout everywhere I went."

Witnessing Shaggy's death was one of the most devastating experiences in my young life.

We cleaned house on Saturdays. The dresser and chest of drawers were dusted, and our worn linoleum rugs mopped and waxed as if expecting Sunday company. The rugs showed more rough dark brown patches than their once smooth, colorful floral pattern. We could see stray bobby pins and twisted brown paper hair rollers between the cracks and a hole in the wall behind the fireboard. They had fallen through and couldn't be retrieved.

After the house was cleaned, Saturday became humdrum, and Mo occasionally pulled out her guitar to strike a tune and sing on our porch. She liked "I'll Fly Away." One time, Hazel and my family gathered to listen to music from an old Victrola we'd borrowed from Uncle Ralph. Millie and Gwen danced on the porch and in our yard. Mo smiled as she swayed to Lord Price's "Lawdy Miss Clawdy," sliding her feet about with a worn straw broom as partner. When the Victrola's metal needles became dull, causing the music to drag slowly, we borrowed new needles from Hazel. That day, music was private entertainment between our families.

On every Saturday evening, Mr. Ezell, our only African American businessman, delivered dry cleaning from the cleaners adjacent to the barbershop. Our families were related via his wife on Mo's side, and we attended the same church. Aunt Trina once lived next door to them. When my siblings and I visited, we could walk to the nearby Belmont Drive-In Theater, relax on the grass, and watch at least part of a movie. Others watched from their vehicles. Mr. Ezell always had Daddy's clothes, usually the dress pants he wore daily to work, and an occasional suit. We delighted in seeing Mr. Ezell walking briskly up the hill behind our house. The dimples in his cheeks made it seem he was always smiling. A long, flowing expanse of brown paper protecting the clothes was draped over his shoulder. He and Mo usually conversed briefly before he went on his way.

That brown dry cleaning paper had several uses. Sometimes, Mo spread it over a wet, mopped floor in place of newspaper to keep the floor clean and safe while it was drying. Occasionally, to help with shoe sizes, Mo would trace our feet on the paper and take the cutout pattern to Stowe Mercantile Company in downtown Belmont or a shoe department in Gastonia. We got new shoes if the old ones were too worn to be repaired in the basement shoe shop downtown. We also used the paper to make twisted, brown paper hair rollers and covers for our schoolbooks.

There were several white businessmen who came to our area: the grocery man, the insurance man, the Rawleigh man, the Watkins man, and the candy man. On Saturday evenings in place of our older grocery man, a tall, slender young white man called the grocery boy came. He wore neatly creased khaki pants with a polo shirt to deliver the week's groceries. That included Sunday's dinner. Perishable items were placed in our icebox where, in the summer, a block of ice slowly melted, often lasting until early Monday morning. Saturday's early supper was very casual, sometimes bologna sandwiches, a rare use of light bread, plain pork 'n' beans, or cut-up wieners without the sandwich, or fried potatoes.

Eventually, since our family had grown, the grocery boy had to start delivering on Wednesdays too; the food no longer lasted a full week. Then we'd have a midweek special treat of sweet milk with graham crackers, sometimes with peanut butter. More important than the snack, our five-gallon kerosene can was refilled. Long, wooden matchsticks and kerosene were used daily for lighting lamps and to start fires in the wood stove, the heater in winter, and around the wash pot on washday. We'd buy Rinso or Duz detergent. Sometimes, a stemmed water glass or a thin washcloth took up space in one of the boxes to entice consumers to purchase a particular brand.

The insurance man didn't come often, but when he did, some of us children met him at the bottom of the hill as soon as he parked his car. He'd hand us small, rectangular puzzle cards to search for items hidden in a colorful picture. We'd sometime walk up the hill with him already searching the puzzles.

The Rawleigh man and the Watkins man came only occasionally. The men's cars showed up at different times loaded with various goods: cleaning products, soap, vitamin supplements, cough medicines, salves, spices, and numerous other items for sale. Mo once purchased a large bottle of vanilla extract from one and lemon pie filling from the other. Several other items interested her that she might have the money for the next time.

Of all the business white men who came to our area, the best one was the candy man, Mr. Riley. He brought us sweet goodies. A friendly man, he came up the hill every Thursday evening with boxes of candy he hoped Mo would allow at least one of us to sell for him. It was good candy—Baby Ruths, Butterfingers, and other choices that sold for five cents each, $2.50 a box. The seller received a profit of 50¢, which was always eaten up in candy. The other option was to save up for the premiums—pots and pans and other housewares—Mr. Riley carried in his car. But that was for grown-ups; we preferred the good stuff.

Though we enjoyed the arrangement, there were occasional problems when more candy was eaten than money earned to pay for it. One Thursday, Gwen was short on some of Mr. Riley's money. She visited Aunt Lydia to avoid him. She had to pay the money the following week, and as punishment, Mo didn't allow her to get a new box to sell for a short while. When Rich needed candy money quick, he would entertain some of the white spectators at the Acme Mill baseball game. For coins, he sang a funny song and danced a jig. But oh if only Mo knew; Rich would have been in more trouble than for just being short of money. She would say the whites were laughing at him make a monkey of himself, looking and sounding foolish. We didn't tell her.

There was one unforgettable time when I was the one with the shortage of candy money. Over several days, I had eaten more candy than I had money for. I told myself each piece would be the last.

By Thursday, I was a nervous wreck. Mr. Riley was going to be coming up that hill expecting his money, and there I was, 45¢ short. On Sunday mornings, Daddy gave us spending money. Some I'd given in Sunday school, and the rest I'd spent for ice cream at the Esso Filling Station. That week, I wished I had saved some money for Thursday. When Mr. Riley came, I was so embarrassed that I cried. Even though Mo didn't have a lot of money to spend on candy or our mistakes, she paid Mr. Riley. Later, she told me he'd looked so pitiful, so disappointed that she couldn't not give him his money. As for me, I was given a second chance as I promised I had learned my lesson.

Sometimes, we sold Moon Pies, cookies, penny candy, and bubble gum instead of candy bars. Mr. Riley was nowhere around when Rich found a partially wrapped piece of gum with a tiny worm in the middle crease. Knowing I had a mouth full of the still sweet, tasty treat, he made sure I saw the worm. I was right in the middle of trying to blow a big bubble when Rich laughed like crazy.

I suddenly shot that gum from my mouth onto the grass. That was just as bad as biting one of Hazel's apples and after chewing a big mouthful noticing a hole. You couldn't help but wonder what had happened to the worm.

We soon discovered other candy had little creatures living on them too. Mo told us not to eat anymore from the boxes of stale goodies. Instead, we saved everything for Mr. Riley.

On Thursday, he was apologetic and innocent, maybe. So we agreed to continue to sell for him; we forgave him but were cautious. The following Thursday, someone yelled, "Here comes Mr. Riley! Here comes the candy man!" And life was back to normal.

Late that summer, Cassie and I made stick playhouses in the same shady area where we'd held our Easter egg hunt. Unlike the spring area, which had a thick layer of low-growing plants, there were brown, dead leaves, pine needles, and rotten, fallen branches under the trees. We used small, leafy branches to sweep the ground of debris and create elaborate flat houses. We used straight sticks for walls and open space for door openings. (In hindsight, those were rustic house plans on the ground rather than on paper.) For decorations, we collected several long stems of Queen Anne's lace and stuck them in old soda bottles.

Playing Miss Lady, we visited each other and chatted like grown-ups with colored dolls that had black, glued-on cotton hair. We served one another rabbit tobacco, crumbled, dry weeds to resemble coffee grounds, and mud pies made in jelly jar lids. Once, prior to leaving our cozy spot for supper, I found a faded orange egg left over from Easter. I took it home and ate it, never thinking it might make me sick. Remarkably, it didn't. After only a few more visits to our playhouses, a copperhead drove us away; it had a family too.

Once in the grassy area of our yard, Mo and Hazel constructed a walk-in playhouse with old wood slabs and complete with a gable roof. For a time, Hazel's girls played there with Cassie and me. Unfortunately, numerous conflicts forced us to stop using it. To our dismay, it was eventually torn down.

Occasionally on Saturday afternoons, Mo caught the city bus to town to purchase items she couldn't find at Joe Farrington's dry goods store; she'd leave Millie and Gwen in charge. One day, Rich and Gwen made the foolish decision to play a dangerous game of catch with Daddy's long and pointed barbering shears. He caused an injury that could've been potentially serious. Mo was livid when she gathered the details. Rich's punishment was forthcoming. Sometimes before and at the end of his whipping, Mo would say she was trying to make a good boy out of him. Rich disliked hearing that since it was always linked to punishment.

Closer to our backyard and diagonally to the back edge of Miss Emma's was a honey locust tree with fruit we called loakry instead of locust. It had a smooth, leathery, textured skin. As long as we didn't see a worm, it was good, like licking a tiny bit of syrup from a hard, flattened, black banana. As far as I was concerned, worms could ruin anything including the rock-hard, wild hickory nuts we gathered by the path to Acme Road and cracked open with a hammer. But worse were the numerous large, fuzzy caterpillars that fell from the oak trees along the path. They made me anxious because I'd probably be oblivious to one landing on me and getting into my hair without warning. All worms were quiet and sneaky; there was something about the way they moved. Their bodies traveled ever so gently going somewhere it was hard to keep track of. And if one got on me, I'd scream as if I'd seen a snake.

Miss Dexter was an elderly white woman who lived with her husband. Though I'd heard his name mentioned, I don't recall ever seeing him. Nevertheless, I knew his wife must've had help with all those cows. I only remember getting a glimpse of her once from a distance. Several of us were on the outside of her pasture on the red-clay roadway. She was wearing a white bonnet and apron over a light blue, below-the-calf cotton dress. The front of her house faced the main street where we played games with passing cars on some Sundays. Miss Cranford's neighborhood and the abbey were on that same street. The rear of her house was enclosed by the vast barbed-wire pasture that extended along the roadway near Hazel's yard, the spring, and the back of the Cranfords. I vaguely remember Mr. Otis, our backyard neighbor, in faded bib overalls coming down our roadway with a pail of fresh milk he'd purchased from the Dexters. Otherwise, to my knowledge, no one else in our four houses had a relationship with the farmers perhaps because we were all African American. But at least once, Cassie, Rich, and I ate wonderful, Golden Delicious apples from one of their trees in the pasture. Neither Miss Dexter nor her husband needed to see us that day. And our parents wouldn't have approved of what we'd done since the fruit was in an enclosed area.

I don't know why we were in her pasture on another occasion, but we were startled by one of her light-brown cows lying on its side stiff and dead just outside the barn. Her stomach was huge, possibly with a baby calf. Her opened eye was the prettiest, big brown eye with long eyelashes I had ever seen. Rich informed Miss Dexter.

Sometime later, the Dexters no longer lived there, and the white farmhouse became a restaurant. We could buy the best doughnuts from a small side window. Following church and dinner one Sunday afternoon, Rich, Cassie, Carl, and I took a shortcut through the pasture. Like sweet, aromatic vanilla and cinnamon clouds floating through the trees, the rich smell of fresh doughnuts filled the air as we approached the restaurant. At the service window, an African American woman bent her head to the opening to take our order. She was our cousin working in a restaurant's kitchen where we couldn't have gone to eat even if we could have afforded it.

I could smell other wonderful meat and vegetable scents. And through the small opening, I saw smooth, white linen tablecloths and shiny silverware adorning several tables. White customers who drove from the main street and parked out front sat and ate there. My cousin just smiled, staring at us four African American children as we collected our thoughts. We just wanted doughnuts.

## Chapter 14

# WILD MILLIE AND RIDICULE

When I was ten, I had my first real crush on a cute boy with pretty round eyes and a nice smile that showed his dimples. He was in the other fifth-grade class, and I looked for him in line at the sweet shop or in the cafeteria. Still shy and remembering my other embarrassment in third grade, I vowed he'd never find out about my feelings.

Millie was quite different. Though growing up and changing, she was quiet, easygoing, and seemingly innocent. At home, she was cooperative and mild mannered, but her classmates and siblings could always tell when she liked a boy or had a boyfriend. Not at all shy, she was open and friendly with the opposite sex. Millie was not above fighting to defend herself the time she was accused of taking someone's boyfriend. We learned this fact one day after school. Millie was short compared to her tall, skinny opponent, but both had long, sharp fingernails (my sister liked using nail polish and kept her nails looking good). They got in a fight just as the bus stopped to let us off for home. Cassie and I were about to begin the walk to our house when I heard excited talking and screaming from the bus. I turned back and stared in awe as I watched through an open window. As the two fought, loud, exciting screams blared from student spectators. Both girls' hair was in disarray, a funny sight as their arms flew in the air and boisterous accusations flew from their mouths. I had never seen teenagers try to settle a dispute like that much less my docile sister.

My view from outside the bus showed the attacks were only on the girls' upper bodies; I saw no kicking. Consequently, Millie came away with only a few scratches on her arms. Gwen said that our sister had defended herself, but all I knew was that without injured legs, Millie was able to walk home.

We were all speechless knowing Millie would have another duel with Daddy when Mo told him. He made it clear to Millie no boy was worth fighting over and he wasn't ever to hear of such a thing happening again. But my siblings and I knew Millie had been getting into trouble ever since she started liking boys. Even Mo called Millie boy crazy and told her she was getting too wild. Besides, acting like that just didn't look good for any girl. Mo added that as a decent young lady, she should have some breathing room in her sweaters and a little extra room in her straight skirts.

Once when Millie was visiting a cousin who lived near the barbershop and Reid High, Daddy caught her with a cigarette in her mouth. When he got after her, she said, "Mo know I smoke Kools." This was far from true, and anyway, she was smoking a Winston. Saying it was a Kool, a milder, menthol cigarette, was supposed to save her, but it didn't.

At home that night, Millie feared Daddy's harsh warnings when he declared that all his chaps were going to be decent. He added he'd better not ever hear of her smoking again. In the end, he agreed with Mo; Millie was out of control. It would take Daddy to tame that side of her that wanted to be free. The same rules would apply to Gwen and the rest of us girls. I learned our parents' expectations from my older sisters' experiences.

Gwen liked boys too, but neither she nor Millie was officially dating at this time. However, one Friday night, Gwen's classmate, who we called her boyfriend, visited her at our house. Really, though, he visited the whole family. Beginning in the ninth grade, students, including Gwen's friend, from Rollins Elementary in Mount Holly, the small town north of Belmont, enrolled at Reid High; they weren't allowed to attend the white high school near their homes. The friend was very neatly dressed and well mannered. He also told us many interesting tales. Unfortunately, he talked so long that he missed the last bus and had to sleep seated backward in a ladder-back chair in our front room. The rest of us slept in the beds. Daddy understood; he accepted the situation as he was too tired from work to drive him the few miles home. The boyfriend left very early the next morning before the rest of us awoke.

Along with expecting our good behavior, my father continuously emphasized the importance of a good education. He didn't want any of us to get sidetracked with other interests such as boys or too much fun and freedom. When Daddy realized Gwen could use additional resources for school assignments, he bought her a brand-new set of *Funk & Wagnall Encyclopedias*, which most of us shared. The cost was worth it, he'd said, since his ultimate plan was for us to have college educations.

Throughout the years, Daddy was still adamant about our connection with church. That was where "Jesus Keep Me Near the Cross," "Pass Me Not O' Gentle Savior," and "Blessed Assurance" became embedded in my head. Mo enjoyed and sang at home, "Just a Closer Walk with Thee"; I liked that as well. Two of my favorite songs were "Just as I Am" and "In the Garden." When I heard the latter, I pictured myself there meeting Jesus. How could I not?

I have only vague memories of the church during the years before I began school. That song also reminded me of the large potbelly stove that sat in the front of the church. Next to it sat the oldest, most frail, and baldest man I'd ever seen. As I eyed him on a pew diagonally across from me, his appearance was unique, almost scary. He was a contrast to the picturesque words in the inviting hymn. As I observed while the congregation sang the song, I probably connected the elderly man with the lyrics. Maybe I felt he needed comfort from the garden while the dew was still on the roses.

Or maybe he just needed warmth from the stove. I don't remember when I no longer saw him.

Aside from his family, job, and church, Daddy had another serious preoccupation: the Brooklyn Dodgers. He and his customers watched the game on TV in the barbershop. The joke was that if the team scored in the middle of a haircut, the man in the barber's chair had better check his head for a mistake. The sole barber in the shop for years, Daddy was very skillful. But if he did blunder, well, hair grew back.

In late spring, Reid High's entire student body participated in a beautiful May Day celebration. Each class was dressed uniformly in colorful spring attire as they performed dances to music on the ball field. One class wrapped the May pole with long, colorful streamers as students performed timed steps.

Finally, school let out for the summer of '55, and inevitably, Hazel shortened our time of fun and relaxation between chores by stirring up trouble. One hot day, I waited under her shady apple tree for Phyllis to come out to play. Hazel said the girls had to clean the kitchen first, so I just stood there watching as she hung her last few wet garments on the far end of her clothesline. When Hazel was done, she placed the empty washtub near me then wiped sweat from her forehead with the back of her hand and forearm. She paused, putting hands on her hips as if to think of what else she had to do. Appearing exhausted, she wandered to her steps to rest. I stayed where I was waiting.

"Tricie," Hazel suddenly said after staring at me, "I b'lieve your thighs are the same size as your legs." Then she smiled as if my legs were an interesting discovery. *Hadn't she noticed them before? I wondered. Did they just change? Is something wrong with my legs?* I wanted to cover them. I always wore shorts in the summer, so I couldn't hide them no more than I could crawl into the ground like a worm into one of her apples.

"I don't know," I said, not knowing how else to respond. "When Phyllis comes out, we're gonna play jack rocks."

Soon, Phyllis and Barbara came out, and Cassie joined us to play jacks with small rocks and a little red ball on our porch. Now and then, I was distracted; I was concerned about my legs. Later that evening, I talked to Gwen, who explained that everyone in our family had legs shaped like mine. The shape came from Mo's side of the family and Daddy's, too. As a man, his calves were just bigger, more muscular. She further explained some people had fat thighs with little legs, but nobody in our family was fat.

"Ain't noth'n wrong with your legs, Tricia," she concluded, making me feel better.

Near the end of the summer, Phyllis and I were playing "O Mary Mack" in her front yard while Mo chatted with Hazel. As we ended the game, I noticed Hazel staring at me.

"Maggie, look at Tricie's eyelashes and eyebrows. You can barely see 'em." She paused, gawking at me. "Almost can't tell she got any."

Mo turned to look, but it was Hazel who made me uncomfortable as if I had undergone a sudden and drastic change. Well, I had—my brown skin with reddish tones had become a couple of shades darker in the summer sun. But that happened every year.

"Look, there's hardly any difference in her skin, her hair, eyebrows, and eyelashes; they all look the same color," Hazel continued. When she noticed my sister and Barbara playing in the yard, she exclaimed, "Look at Cassie's and Barbara's dark eyebrows and eyelashes."

Mo wouldn't dispute Hazel, so she didn't defend me. But I didn't like being compared to Cassie or Barbara. Uncomfortable, I went inside our house. *I must be very ugly to Hazel*, I thought. *First my legs and thighs, and now my eyebrows and eyelashes? Why did she have to make fun of parts of me over which I have no control?*

That night, I wasn't ready to get in bed for a while. Thanks to Hazel, I had taken on a horrible view of myself. I struggled to find something positive about my looks. The light was dim, and the flame was flaring since again there was no replacement globe for the kerosene lamp. I sat at the dresser staring into the mirror while most of the family slept. My eyes would never be as beautiful as that dead cow's. But Cou'n Tilley had called me a pretty little girl with big, pretty, brown eyes. Well, Cou'n Tilley had died last year, so I couldn't expect to hear those kind words from her again. I didn't want to see her again either.

Continuing to analyze myself, I started to feel worthless. I knew many people liked me, grown-ups and friends at school. Maybe they and my teachers thought I was ugly. In a rage, my attitude must've been, "If you want to see ugly, I'll show you ugly! This new look will be worse than how you saw me before!" I began to pull out my top eyelashes, some more difficult than others. I felt a little sting when each tug was successful. My arm was cramped by the time I had plucked out about a third from each eye. I didn't care how I'd look in the morning; it couldn't be any worse than I felt. Finally, I gave up, and finding my spot among my siblings, went to sleep.

When I awoke, no one seemed to notice that I was truly different now. Neither did I say anything though I hurt terribly inside.

# Chapter 15

## THE PARK AND THE PROMISE—GRADE 6

It took me a long time to realize that by eating fresh onions with his pinto beans on Mondays, his day off, Daddy was ensuring his customers wouldn't have to tolerate onion breath.

Instead of a bowl, he always ate his beans on a plate. On pleasant afternoons, he sometimes sat next to the big flat rock, his outside table, across from our former kitchen window. Once when I was playing in the area, Daddy called me over to talk. He ate his beans and sipped water. He wore dress pants with tan suspenders over a crisp, white, short-sleeve shirt Mo had starched and ironed. I knew he was serious by the way he addressed me.

"Tricie Ann, when you were born, I got a furlough from Fort Bragg to come home." He glanced at me as I stood watching him eat. Then he went on to explain that because Mo was expecting me, she'd taken Millie, Gwen, and Rich to stay with Aunt Gernie and Uncle Pete.

I had heard the story of my birth several times usually from Mo. However, Daddy had difficulty completing the part about his war experiences in West Germany. I assumed by his facial expression it must've been a sad story. Nevertheless, he quickly completed his meal.

I turned eleven that summer. During the day, my siblings and I had fun sometimes including the Simpson children. On Tuesday evenings, both families looked forward to going to Stowe Park, a large amusement park in downtown Belmont. Tuesday was African American night. We took our baths and dressed in clean, comfortable clothes well in advance so we'd be ready when Daddy's customer and friend came to pick us up. He always had a small, brown paper bag or white tied handkerchief of change for Mo to purchase refreshments and tickets for rides.

At the park, there were so many lights that the huge central area glowed bright like day. Music from the rides, especially the merry-go-round, filled the air with excitement. Nearby, a large, round concrete dance floor with a jukebox filled with updated music and rhythms added to the atmosphere. Along with other refreshments, soft-serve ice cream, popcorn, drinks, and cotton candy were available. Tickets for rides were 10¢, and all was sold through a small window in the concession building. As soon as we arrived, we rode the Ferris Wheel and the train that circled most of the park blowing its horn when going through a tunnel. Some teenage couples stole kisses.

In addition to the rides, we sometimes paid to play putt-putt, or carpet golf. It required much of our time to complete as did the free movie shown in a secluded area near the main entrance. Popular movies were screened at the amphitheater, the starlit sky above. There was also a wide variety of free play equipment large and small, a wading pool we didn't use, and separate restrooms for African Americans. We had to be careful not to get lost from our families because the park was always packed with locals and visitors from surrounding cities. All were eager to take advantage of that one weekly night. Whites attended all other nights except Sundays, when the park was closed.

One night around 10:00, closing time, all the lights went off at the park. Downtown Belmont was dark, too since the stores had closed hours before. I was waiting with my family at the main entrance for our ride to take us home as on all other Tuesday nights.

Practically everyone had left. The last few cars were pulling off. We were exhausted; my youngest siblings were sleepy and whiny. Unfortunately, Mo had no way to communicate with Daddy. When our ride failed to show, we walked home, the older ones carrying the younger ones as we took the shortcut through the abbey. We hoped there were no snakes along the weedy path before reaching the roadway between the two pastures to our house.

By the time all nine of us reached our chinaberry tree, Daddy was walking up the hill behind our house. Startled by our silhouettes and light conversation, he was very apologetic. He had forgotten to send a ride to take us home so we could rest and savor our evening's enjoyment.

One day, Hazel came over to tell Mo she had been offered a job in a café kitchen in downtown Belmont. Mo was excited for her, saying we could all use a little more money. But Hazel wasn't done. Nervously twisting her hands together, she asked Mo about looking after her chaps a few hours each day. Hazel must've known this was a lot to ask a mother with eight children. However, to keep the peace, Mo didn't outright say no.

"Well, I guess it'll be all right with Millie and Gwen helping out," she said, clearly hesitant to commit to such responsibility.

"Maggie, that's just what I was thinking!" Hazel ignored Mo's discomfort. "You'll have some help, and Phyllis and Barbara can almost take care of themselves. So, it'll be mostly Li'l Stevie. He'll play with Dan, and I can give you something for your trouble though I won't be making much."

Hearing that conversation from my seat in our tire swing, I recalled the conflicts that arose whenever we interacted or played with Hazel's children. Only their point of view was believed; Hazel rarely trusted Mo's attempts at explanation.

That night, when Mo talked with Daddy, he was angry.

"Maggie, you ought to know what you're getting yourself into! Hazel gets a check. That's not enough?"

He knew that Hazel, who was unmarried with three children and no job, received a monthly government check to support her and her family. He also knew that if Hazel worked while receiving financial help, she would be in trouble with the law. Mo didn't need to have any part in that. Besides, he was well aware of our constant conflicts with Hazel; she just meant trouble. Nevertheless, Mo's decision was made. She'd have to learn for herself without more discussion with Daddy.

The following night, Daddy had better things to talk about such as how well he was doing saving money for our new house. He knew Mo's babysitting arrangement would end with the summer. Anyway, as long as it didn't storm, the Simpson children could play out in the yard and not be squeezed inside under Mo's feet. If it rained, our porch was enough shelter. Cassie and I promised to be cautious with the Simpson girls knowing we'd have to be together the next day and the next.

A couple of weeks later, when all were playing in our yard, someone spotted a tall, skinny white woman coming up the hill. We stared because no white woman had ever been seen in our African American area. Nor did she look like the plain mill workers we were used to. She was dressed up with bright-red lipstick. Her dark, shoulder-length hair was brushed shiny and smooth. At first, we thought she was coming to our house, but she veered right to take the path to Hazel's instead. We all knew Hazel wasn't home when we watched the woman go around the corner to her door. Momentarily, she came to our yard to speak with Millie while several inquisitive children gathered around them.

"I'm Mary Thornberg," she said. "I'm looking for Hazel Simpson."

Before Millie could respond, Stevie spoke up, offering his friendly help. "My mama's gone 'a work," he blurted out.

"Aren't you a sweetie!" The woman smiled and bent down to him.

By the time Mo came out, there was no more to say other than introductions.

"It's nice meeting you, Miss Littleton. I was looking for Hazel

Simpson, but it seems I have found only her children. Have a good day. Bye bye." She gave a little wave, smiled, and was off.

When Hazel stopped by after work, Mo told her about the visit. The news disturbed Hazel. She still wasn't her usual self the next day when she came by with her children. Mo brushed off Hazel's moodiness, saying she must have been tired.

That afternoon, I sat lazily in the swing, my bare feet scraping the warm, red clay as I kicked a few fallen chinaberries to a grassy patch. A couple of my siblings were lingering nearby. Hazel and my mother stood between the two yards talking grown-up talk we weren't supposed to hear.

"Y'all, go'n out yonder and play! Have some manners!"

I'd heard that command many times, as it was considered bad manners for children to eavesdrop around adults. But that day, I wasn't pretending not to hear; I was just swinging. As their conversation continued, Hazel became animated; she flung her arms in all directions. Her facial expression was strained and her attitude frightening. I wasn't sure whether to stay put or go in my house to alert my older siblings. I steadied the swing to listen and watch.

"How we gonna eat?" Hazel shouted. "How am I supposed to feed my family without a check?" She moved off to her own yard passing her kitchen window. Though sometimes she dipped snuff, she lit a cigarette and nervously puffed away at it as she sat on the top step. And as usual, she arranged her drab, cotton housedress between her knees, bare feet exposing the day's filth. Her head was cocked to one side. I watched as she blew smoke away from Mo, who had followed and stood facing her. *This is a time Mo should be coming home*, I thought, *not moving closer.*

Mo was never firm or aggressive with Hazel, whom she'd expressed to us had to be handled delicately—like a rotten egg. Instead, Mo was easygoing and eager to make amends. On the other hand, Hazel's mood was often a reflection of what was in or not in her pocketbook. But Mo too had children to feed. When Hazel again blamed her for not getting a check, I knew she had accused my mother of something awful.

Confident she had established fear in Mo and had left her defenseless, Hazel took a final puff on her Pall Mall. She flicked the butt past Mo toward a grassy clay area across from her kitchen window. Barely allowing Mo to speak, she stormed up from the step and disappeared into her kitchen, the ragged screen door slamming loudly behind her. Seeing Mo's timid expression, I felt it was unfair for a much younger woman to have so much power over and lack of respect for my mother.

I discreetly relayed to my older siblings what I had heard and seen. We agreed Mo had more to say to defend herself. It didn't happen that day though. Instead, she came home and went directly to the kitchen to be alone. The rest of the afternoon was solemn as Mo began preparing supper and limiting conversation, revealing nothing regarding Hazel. We knew it was no ordinary controversy but a serious grown-up issue.

By the time Daddy came home from the barbershop, we were all in bed. It was after ten o'clock. I didn't hear him come in though he had to pass through the house where most of us slept to get to the kitchen. Adjusting myself in bed, I listened as Mo fixed Daddy's plate and prepared their rollaway bed. At first, all I could hear was his silverware hitting his plate and his smacking loudly through the closed door as he gobbled down his late supper. Mo despised Daddy's eating habits especially when he talked between chewing his food. Normally she let him know it, but that time, she was tolerating it. She needed reassurance.

Daddy stopped eating. "Maggie, that woman is crazy! I keep telling you don't mess with her! You need to just stay away from her! She's trouble, nothing but trouble!"

Daddy's outburst got my full attention, and the others stirred beside me in bed.

Mo knew it was easy for him to say she should stay away from Hazel because he was usually gone all day and part of the night. Being away from home eliminated the stress of dealing with Hazel and her children. Most important, he didn't have to tolerate all Mo had to in order to keep harmony with her almost daily.

I heard a faint whisper from Mo. Then Daddy raised his voice again. "We're not always gonna be living like this!"

As he ate, Mo tried to explain her concern, saying, "Nat, I couldn't believe what Hazel said to me. She thinks I—"

"I promise you one day this will be over," Daddy said in a matter-of-fact tone. "We're gonna have a nice house, and you and the chaps won't have to take shortcuts across Hazel's yard anymore." He scraped his plate loudly. "We'll have real lights, electricity …" He paused as if meeting her eyes to show his sincerity. "Stop worrying. Our chaps won't have to live in this cramped house for long. They won't have to depend on people like Hazel to make 'em happy. I just need a little more time. Trust me, Maggie."

Mo didn't trust Daddy; she was about sick of his empty promises. Throughout the years, he'd occasionally shared with her his thoughts of a future bigger house for our family. In talking with us about "way back," Mo had sometimes shared his seemingly wishful thinking. Though Daddy tried to convince her he was saving money for our new house, he'd been making that same promise since Rich was born. Bringing it up at that time, he evaded her immediate problem. Instead, he saw only his role in changing our family's future. Moving us to a better house would rid us of Hazel. To Mo, Daddy was feeling guilty for forcing us to live in that house in the first place. The birth of each child had sent him a little deeper in a hole he only then felt confident about pulling us out of. Except Mo wasn't concerned about our future; she needed her husband's help for the next day. I had difficulty putting together the pieces of these two very separate issues: Daddy's plans and Mo's immediate problem with Hazel.

Soon, the kerosene lamp in the kitchen was blown out. Only muttering snuck around the door frame. In complete darkness in my narrow, sweaty space in our big bed, I listened to the round white clock on the fireboard softly ticking. I relaxed, relieved of the day's tensions as I fell into a deep slumber and the night drifted away.

## Chapter 16

# NEW TEACHERS, NEW BEGINNINGS

As a change from what I was beginning to see as my worse summer ever thanks to Hazel, I eagerly awaited the start of school. Sixth grade would be good. Fresh from the military, two new male teachers had arrived at Reid High. Wearing suits or sport coats and dress pants, neckties, and shiny shoes, they looked very professional. One of them would be my teacher.

Mr. Hunter was a medium-built, dark-skinned man with well-groomed hair. He smiled a lot, showing dimpled cheeks and a gap between his top front teeth. His gentle and caring voice was just what I needed after hearing Hazel's critical and harsh tones throughout the summer.

The class liked and respected our teacher, who shared with us some of his military experiences. When he taught us music singing with a gleam in his eyes, snapping his fingers, and patting his foot to the rhythm, we sang, "The White Cliffs of Dover" and other songs. Mr. Hunter felt like a father away from home, which was especially nice since I didn't see Daddy that much during the school year.

"What's the matter, Patty?" he sometimes asked.

Patty was the nickname Mr. Hunter had given me, but I don't recall ever discussing a problem with him. He made me feel better simply by asking. I was still pulling out my eyelashes, but I didn't expect he could help me with that. I pulled them out, they grew back, and the habit continued.

On a cool school night in early fall, the family attended the county fair about twenty-seven miles west of Belmont. Just as for the amusement park, Daddy sent a customer to transport Mo and all eight of us children in our family car, young siblings sitting on older ones' laps. There were crowds of whites and African Americans there enjoying the tiring night of fun and excitement.

That fall, we began hearing serious talk about our future home. Mo said Daddy no longer spent his money foolishly and had started saving for a new house to be built near Reid High. He'd purchased a parcel of land. We needed space and privacy, desires Daddy had had for several years though Mo had doubted he would ever accomplish them.

Toward Christmas, our northern section of Belmont came alive with an animated scene on Acme Mill's flat rooftop across from our school bus stop. All lit up after dark, it was a cozy, family scene with a fire in the fireplace and a grandma knitting in a rocking chair. A young child sat at her feet while Santa was perched to come down the chimney. On our way to Uncle Ralph's, we sometimes detoured to stand on the mill's manicured lawn in the cold to enjoy the display of life-sized props. Occasionally, we walked to the mill to get out of the house during the weekend as well. Light traffic on the street behind us slowed; others were enjoying the scene as we dreamed about our future home.

Christmas came and went with the usual excitement. We were all thankful and happy about our gifts. Rich had long wanted a BB gun, a gift that proved to be a mistake. He was caught shooting at the Jackson's toilet after several girls rushed toward it. We all knew there was only one seat. Consequently, Rich was forced to switch his focus back to slingshots. Cassie and I received similar wool hats with flaps to cover our ears and ties for under our chins. Cassie's was Christmas green while mine was bright red. We prolonged the Christmas celebration all winter by wearing our red and green hats.

We wore them when together we went to the school bus stop, the store, and church instead of our usual headscarves. (I didn't like the way mine looked on, and so I wore it with the bib propped up to improve my appearance, or so I thought. Family members tried to tell me it looked stupid, but I wasn't convinced.)

The year before, Andrea had been only a couple of months old, too young to take it all in. That Christmas, she enjoyed the chatter and excitement of siblings with gifts as she clutched a soft, brown baby doll Santa brought just for her. Like my younger siblings before her, Andrea was a special joy especially when she was small and cuddly. By that time, she had become my real walking doll. I could hold her hand and she'd walk along trusting me. With ten years between us, I felt comfortable watching after her, not just feeding her a bottle of milk as I'd done when she was younger.

Uncle Ed still visited us sometimes during the day or evening. The whole family recognized his playful knock on our unlatched door: "Da, da, da, da, da ... da, da!" Like any other visitor, we were always glad to see him. He must've been like Rich when he was a boy—mischievous though with a somewhat annoying sense of humor. If any of us was in bed sleeping, our bare feet exposed, Ed delighted in lightly tickling them with a small piece of paper, laughing and watching us squirm. Or he'd take a book of matches from his pocket, place a match between our toes, and light it. He waited for us to yell out as he chuckled. That was a hot foot.

Ed also found it amusing to use Millie's or Gwen's red nail polish to write my name on my forehead while I slept. As the polish dried, I scratched my itchy face. When I looked in the mirror the next morning, I saw I'd been labeled as if to learn who I really was. Mo didn't mind his pranks as long as she saw we were unhurt and our house was still standing.

It was often dark when Ed visited during the short days of fall and winter. Mo often cooked sweet potatoes as a less-rich version of candied yams, or she'd rub several with margarine or butter before baking them. I preferred them cold; I liked eating one the next day. She also made sweet potato pies and sweet potato cobblers, my favorite. But it was the simple candied yams Ed usually asked about. "Hey, Puddy." He playfully called Mo pretty. "Got any of those sweet ones?"

Usually, everybody had eaten by then except Daddy, and Mo would tell Ed to help himself. He'd put some on a small dish to eat, usually standing, his legs crossed as he leaned one shoulder against the door frame, washing it down with spring water.

We were an outlet within walking distance and away from his isolated environment of three mill houses. All the same, he didn't stay very long when he visited. Since my father's siblings, Aunt Thelma, Uncle Ralph, and Ed, were all members of O'Conner's Grove Church, we saw them at least weekly. However, they had another brother, Uncle Sam, who lived in the community close to Reid High and the barbershop. He attended a nearby church; unfortunately, we seldom saw him or his family.

One Saturday morning in early spring when Daddy was about to leave for work, Mo shared some exciting news. The builder had started our new house. That prompted smiles everywhere and questions about when we could move in.

"Oh it'll take months before it's finished." Daddy smiled as if to say, "Maggie, see? I tried to tell you so, but I knew you didn't believe me."

A couple of weeks later after Sunday dinner, we went to see the beginnings of our house. The foundation was complete and framing was progressing. It was amazing, and we all were so proud that Daddy had kept his promise to Mo. He'd stayed focused on his goal. And even though it had been delayed for years, this large, soon-to-be-brick house would be the result of his perseverance. There was a lot to smile about and much to absorb.

We all had new hopes and thoughts of new ways of living. We'd have electricity and water. We'd have an upstairs, a downstairs, and a basement! We'd have closets! Best of all, Hazel would soon be history. Though we'd have to continue handling her like that rotten egg Mo talked about until we moved, it helped knowing our dream of moving was finally becoming a reality.

Before Easter, Cassie and I made a special trip through the woods to Miss Cranford's neighborhood. Cou'n Marcus had built a fabulous brick house for him and his wife like movie stars on television. Cou'n Jackie had promised to pierce our ears. She'd use ice cubes to deaden our ear lobes before pushing the needle with white doubled thread through. She formed a short loop and knotted and clipped the thread. At home, we used alcohol to keep the area clean, and we used Vaseline to keep the threads turning easily and maybe helped with healing. Then we wore our first pair of earrings, one little dangling bird per ear. Mine had red gemstone eyes while Cassie's had blue. Wearing earrings, we felt like our big sisters.

Saying we had to cut back on money for Easter outfits, Mo took Cassie and me on the bus to Gastonia. She purchased some blue and white gingham for Cassie and green and white for me. At home, she made us pleated jumpers with jackets under which we would wear lace-trimmed, white blouses. Frilly hats would adorn our heads, and thin socks with black patent-leather slippers decked our feet.

Gwen and Millie were hoping for new, store-bought clothing, but Mo said new clothes weren't what Easter was really about. She shared her decision with Daddy and reminded us all that this was a good way to save money for the new house and its furnishings. Then a week or so before Easter, she discovered two new suits, a dressy gray one and a seersucker one Daddy had purchased and left hidden in the trunk of our car. Mr. McAlbe's wife had opened a new ladies' clothing store adjacent to the grocery store where all we had to say was, "Charge to Nat Littleton." In a snap, Mo sent Millie to purchase three outfits—one for her, Gwen, and Millie, all charged to Daddy.

On Easter morning, Daddy was stunned when he saw how lovely his wife and older daughters looked in their new clothes. They were as pretty as he was handsome in his new gray suit. He stared and obviously wanted to say something, but Mo beat him to it. "I see you like that gray suit better than the seersucker one." She smiled and left the room.

No, Daddy didn't complain. He couldn't. Guilt was all over his face.

In late spring, the National Junior Honor Society hosted a fun hayride and picnic in Gastonia. Cassie and I had earned good grades and were proud members. Like most students, we packed our lunches for the day in shoeboxes. We had bologna sandwiches, store-bought chocolate chip cookies, and bananas still ripening. They flavored everything. It was interesting to hike through unfamiliar woods to discover a different creek and experience nature on a beautiful new trail.

I had been right; sixth grade was good not only at school but at home as well. The news of our rapidly progressing house construction was exhilarating. Excited, Daddy talked of his hopes to move in late summer, possible by August. Mo showed the same enthusiasm Rich, Cassie, and I did when we talked about our Christmas lists. She said we'd never have to wait in the cold for the bus again because we'd be able to walk the two blocks to school. And if necessary, Daddy could walk three blocks to the barbershop or even a shorter distance if he took a shortcut. Mo never said we wouldn't have to deal with Hazel; that was understood. The rest of the world always seemed at peace while my family and I were at war with Hazel. We weren't certain how we'd survive just one more summer.

# Chapter 17

## THREATS AND ANOTHER STORM

During the summer of '56, Hazel was more irate than ever. After Hazel had seen the builder discussing the blueprints with Daddy in our front yard, Mo had told her about our house. We braced ourselves for her tantrums. Our angry neighbor refused to allow Mo and the rest of us to enjoy the remaining time leading to our long-anticipated move.

It was a Wednesday, a light washday. Mo was scrubbing a small load of clothes on our porch near the rock steps as she sometimes did. While I sat on the other end sucking my lip and fondling my neck, Phyllis entered our yard. Completely ignoring me, she walked directly up to Mo. "Miss Maggie," she said, "Mama wants you to come 'nere."

With no comment or change in facial expression, Mo dried her sudsy hands on the sides of her old wash dress. Hazel knew any washday was tiring, heavy or light. There must be an urgent matter brewing. Mo told Gwen and Millie to try to finish the load of clothes, adding that I'd have to help get more rinse water.

Hazel met her in her yard by the kitchen window. "Why did you have to tell Miss Thornberg I wuz working?" she screamed in Mo's face. "Why, Maggie?"

Mo was stunned. "Hazel, I didn't tell that lady anything. Why would you think that?"

"Yes you did! She would o' axed you!"

"I told you she was leaving when I met her."

Hazel was furious and screamed Mo was a liar.

"You can ask Millie. Stevie told that lady you went to work, not me." Mo thought the truth would calm Hazel, but her anger was impermeable. As if Mo's composed defense had provoked her, Hazel screamed even louder and called Mo a liar.

Mo was sensitive and often defenseless when anybody spoke harshly to her. Though Daddy sometimes did when he was impatient with her, she could tell him to stop raising his voice. For some reason, she couldn't say the same to Hazel. Neither could she prove her innocence.

Hazel wiped a tear from her eyes and sat on her steps. Mo followed still hoping to settle the misunderstanding.

"You knew how to make things harder for me!" Hazel said. "How we gonna eat? You know where your food's coming from!"

Just as I thought she'd settled down, she suddenly rose from the steps flinging her arms. "Maggie, get out o' my yard!"

Mo came home and continued the wash. Without discussing the matter, she scrubbed a handful of dirty clothes as hard as she could. Sudsy water splashed from the tub onto the porch. Rich, Cassie, and I started for the spring for more water. When we neared Hazel's house, there she was stomping on her porch as if waiting for us.

"Get out o' my yard! Get out! Y'all have to walk around!"

I didn't want to carry heavy buckets a longer distance, but we walked to the wide outer edge where sweet-smelling honeysuckle contrasted with Hazel's anger.

When we told Mo we had to go around Hazel's yard to go to and from the spring, she told us to be cooperative. Like with any adult, we were to be respectful. When we inquired about playing with the Simpson girls, Mo said if they came to our yard, we should play as if nothing had happened. "Play like you been," she said. We knew if we hoped to live peacefully with the Simpsons, there had to continue to be a lot of giving and forgiving from the Littletons.

By the time we finished pouring the water in the washtub, Phyllis, the Simpson messenger, was headed to our yard carrying a white bowl.

"Miss Maggie," she said softly, "Mama said here's yo' eggs she borrowed." She handed Mo the bowl before turning to leave.

"Shucks! Hazel knows she don't have to pay back those eggs," Mo mumbled, shaking her head disgustedly.

Later that day, Phyllis returned. Speaking in the same low tone, she directed her message to Gwen. "Mama said she wants her straightening comb you borrowed."

Gwen got the comb from where it sat on the fireboard next to our Royal Crown Hair Dressing. Handing it to Phyllis, she told her to thank her mother.

It was clear Hazel was only being difficult to show how uneasy she could make a Littleton feel. She was behaving like an immature, grown-up bully.

"I just can't live like this," Mo said numerous times. She was tired of Hazel, who seemed intent on making the rest of our time living next to her feel twice as long.

About a week later, Cassie and I walked barefoot to the store for a couple of household items. When we arrived home, we found the rest of our family in tears on our porch because Hazel had made very frightening threats. My sister and I cried with them. I couldn't imagine our family without Mo, our leader. How could anybody not like her? She was kind and even tempered; she always took time to think rather than reacting brashly during conflict.

We were afraid for our mother to leave our sight. When Mo said she was going to town or anywhere else, we'd all line up to kiss her good-bye.

"Mo, let me kiss you good-bye," we'd say. One by one, we hugged her and gave her a kiss on the cheek. Then we crowded the back window to watch her pass Hazel's house and disappear from sight and Hazel for at least a while.

Hazel was one storm. One night, we had another: a thunderstorm with frightful lightning flashes that turned our dark, hot room into daylight. During any storm, the entire family was always together in our main room. No one dared leave it; we'd sit or lie on our beds. Even with Mo nearby in the big chair, the deafening and seemingly never-ending thunder caused us to jump.

Gwen told her scary story about three brothers who sold tobacco at night in some woods where weird people lived. Uninformed visitors to the area experienced a horrible fate: inside one of the small houses, a huge pot of a peculiar stew sat on a wood stove tended constantly by a strange woman. I don't recall all of the details of the story, but Gwen had told it several times and knew how to embellish it with interesting twists. It distracted us from the thunder and lightning.

Rich shared his story about a ghost he had seen a few years earlier along the path on the far side of our chinaberry tree toward the red-clay roadway. A short, white woman in a long, thin gown and a jacket appeared in broad daylight. She had short, white hair and was bent over a walking stick. After briefly turning away, Rich looked back. She had disappeared. After that, he continuously searched the area knowing she was around, but he never saw her again. I chose to forget that ghost since I along with my siblings frequented the area daily.

Mo had said she thought the storm would "go 'round," but as it continued, we asked her to talk about way back, and she began with the games she and her siblings played outside. One she called Hack Giving, like a game of skills and dares. Each participant tried a stunt to outdo the others. One time, Mo's stunt was so good that she got stuck high in the barn's crib area and couldn't get down. She'd had to wait to be found and helped, which Mo laughed about for years.

Loud, heavy rain splashed on our roof. Mo enjoyed talking about her family and the games and fun they had together as well as the sad times. She expressed her love for her father, whom she called Papa. Though half white, he looked all white just like her grandfather, a white man. Her father was very kind and easygoing just like Mo and with a good sense of humor. He was a good man everybody liked, and Mo had been very close to him. He died early following an injury after falling. She often told the touching story beginning with how he had worked in the abbey bakery after his mill job.

As Mo talked, I could only imagine him climbing on a ladder or stepstool to reach something stored high in a pantry. Losing his balance, he fell to the floor, and heavy items from the shelves crushed his chest. Sadly, Mo said that from then on, a shadow of the Blessed Virgin Mary appeared on the wall by his bed each evening. It moved closer each day until it rested over his head the evening he died.

Mo also talked about her Native American/African American grandmother, a midwife and medicine doctor. She pushed a cart of herbs through Anson County, North Carolina. Uncle Pete, whose house Mo shared when I was born, once described a vision he'd had. A child's head with long, black, straight hair and brown arms appeared in a whirlwind of leaves that blew her down a path in the woods near their home. It quickly disappeared. The family called the vision a token or premonition. Not long after, Mo's grandmother died smiling at a very old age while holding Cou'n Edna on her lap to remove the child's shoes.

Focused on Mo's spooky stories, those of us still awake didn't realize the storm had ended. Light rain and red mud kept our family in for a couple of days. We'd use our water supply sparingly until we could make trips to the spring again.

A few nights later, there was more heavy rain and rumbles of thunder as we fell asleep. By morning, all outside was cool, fresh, and wet. The rain had finally stopped. As the sun forced its way out, one of the first chores was to go to the spring. Rich and I grabbed the water buckets and Cassie came along.

When we reached Hazel's toilet, the path to the spring was muddy. The spring and branch were disastrous. Like a river, they overflowed with red, muddy water that made it difficult to fill our buckets. At home, we'd let the red clay settle to the bottom being careful not to stir it up when dipping. That would have to suffice.

Midmorning the next day, the three of us returned to the spring and saw the overflow had subsided a little. We could safely fill our buckets by following a lower path to the right along the branch rather than going directly downhill from the big tree. Later that evening, we made a second trip. That's when Rich got the brilliant idea to punish Hazel for being so mean to our mother. Following his direction, we poured buckets of water over the clearing and the higher and lower paths just to rewet the surface. Then we glided over the slushy mud barefooted to make it slippery. We wanted to make certain Hazel would have difficulty getting to the spring no matter which route she took. And even if she were able to get there, she'd surely have problems getting back up the hill with her foot tub and bucket of water.

We worked hastily knowing Hazel could catch us in the act. When our mischief was completed, Rich filled our water buckets from over the top of the spring. Prior to starting home, he had to clarify one important detail.

"Y'all know you can't tell Mo. Can't nobody tell! Y'all hear that?"

"I'm not gon' tell," I responded, knowing I would be in big trouble too if I did.

Feeling guilty and slightly afraid but also excited over the prank we hoped to pull off, we returned to the house. When Mo asked what had taken us so long, we explained how difficult it was to get to the water without falling in. The mud between our toes was proof, but that was being dishonest. That was lying. And we knew she wouldn't approve of our behavior because we were doing evil for evil. Somehow, we should instead find it in our hearts to be respectful.

To know when Hazel went to the spring, at least one of us tried to remain outside. We'd sit in the swing or on the big rock out front. We knew her water supply would soon be depleted because our tracks to the spring had been the only ones made that day.

As the sun was going down, Rich spied Hazel in her light green, cotton dress carrying her bucket and foot tub. "There she goes! There she goes!" he discreetly called.

Rich, Cassie, and I waited impatiently. A trip to the spring and back took less than thirty minutes on a dry day. There were two definite rest stops, one by the big oak after coming up the hill from the spring, and another by Hazel's toilet. We allowed her extra time for careful footing along the slippery path. Gwen soon joined us out in the yard, and Rich shared our scheme. We all wanted to see Hazel return with a muddy dress.

At last out of the woods, she appeared by her toilet. We watched as she put her containers down to rest, her hands propped at her waist. Then facing us, she started toward her house. From a safe distance, we examined her carefully but saw no mud on her dress as she neared her steps. That prank was too much hard work to be for nothing. We were disappointed right up until she set the foot tub down and went up her steps with the water bucket. That's when we saw her entire rear end and much of her back covered in a smear of red clay. That was both humorous and frightening. If caught, we knew there would be consequences for our behavior; we'd be in big trouble with Mo. Though Hazel said nothing then, the not knowing when was our punishment.

As my twelfth birthday neared, Mo realized I had never had a special birthday celebration with a cake. After sending Millie and me to town to get all we needed for a simple party, Mo made a cake with white icing and candles. We made homemade vanilla ice cream by taking turns with the crank. Wearing colorful paper birthday hats, the family sang the birthday song to me. We celebrated around an old table covered with a crisp, white sheet placed under the chinaberry tree. I was the star of my extraordinary day.

## Chapter 18

# TURMOIL AND NEW HOUSE—GRADE 7

That summer, O'Conner's Grove became a new church; the white frame building with mullion windows was renovated. It became a modern brick church with stained glass windows. Members purchased windows in honor of their families. Daddy's was labeled to represent Grandma Littleton and their family.

Like a promised whipping, Hazel's silence remained torture. We didn't know when she might storm into our yard yelling at Mo for what we had done. Hazel must have sat in her house conjuring up trouble because every few days she reemerged yelling awful things. I was glad my mother didn't behave like that. Although Hazel's children often stayed inside when she was enraged, I'd still be so embarrassed and ashamed.

Daddy knew Hazel couldn't have it both ways; she needed to obey the law. Either she'd work or she'd receive checks to support herself and her children. We all knew that without anyone to watch them, she'd had to quit her job at the café. I never understood how Mo could have had anything to do with that. She'd only tried to help Hazel regardless of her own overload of responsibilities.

We had family chores to do, including washing clothes and carrying water from the spring, now more dreadful than ever. Therefore, staying safely inside our house was not an option. About a week later, Hazel saw Mo outside. And when Mo again tried to explain her innocence, it again provoked our neighbor. Instead of calming down, she became enraged and threatening.

Watching from our porch with the rest of us, Millie suddenly stomped down in front of Hazel, shocking us all. "Do it then, Hazel! Just do it then!"

I suppose Hazel was just as shocked as we were at mild-mannered Millie. Maybe that fight on the school bus had given my sister confidence. Though Daddy had said she was never to fight over a boy, he'd never said she couldn't use words to protect our mother from Hazel, an adult behaving childishly, if she needed to.

At any rate, Hazel backed off, retreating slowly to her house as her frightened children waited on their steps. Who else but them would want to console her?

No matter the turmoil or what we lacked materially in our house, there would always be many fond memories of our time there. The spring, pastures, woods, and our chinaberry tree were the connecting points in many pleasant family memories. Nevertheless, I could not imagine ever returning to that setting once we moved especially while Hazel still lived there. We subsisted in a secluded, African American area of four houses. The two families at the bottom of the hill were unaware of the discord between the two families at the top. Alone on our chinaberry hill, our two families were divided. In the end, each struggled to survive based on very different circumstances.

Our statuesque chinaberry tree growing on the slope in our front side yard served many purposes over the years. One large branch supported our swing while another held an end of our clothesline. The leafy limbs provided shade throughout the summer and little purple and white flowers in the spring. Later, many of the thousands of little green berries were strung for Cassie's and my jewelry. Come fall and winter, ripened, golden-tan berries hung in clusters making the tree an interesting work of art when the leaves were gone. Rich used the dried berries for his slingshot. Even now, I could draw a replica of our chinaberry tree's largest branches.

In a similar way, the open area of Mr. Shoemaker's pasture was always a source of pleasure. Free of distractions from tall, hovering trees, we chased a rainbow but didn't come out on the losing end when there was no pot of gold, just beauty. We enjoyed the freedom to explore the surrounding woods where we ate all sorts of berries: black, dew, currant, and mulberries.

There were also wild plums, persimmons, wild sumac, honey locust, and muscadines. We enjoyed Asian pears, which we called rusty-core pears, that we found at the pasture's edge when we remembered them. Hazel's tart apples became sweeter in the fall. It was a pleasure to grab one freely from the cool, wet grass after a heavy rain. Miss Dexter had wonderful Golden Delicious apples, which we shouldn't have eaten, and had a house that became a restaurant where we bought delectable doughnuts. After our last and most memorable visit, while Carl was eating one, he was fired up when a yellow jacket flew into his mouth.

Though the move was still weeks off, future changes and thoughts of leaving the area where I'd lived for twelve years were overwhelming. I knew every scrape, crack, and hole inside and outside our current home and every root on the paths to Acme Road and the spring.

On a cool, summer, moonlit evening, several of us including Rich sat on the grassy backyard slope. Just under the big white oak's lower branches, we had a side view of the Jacksons' house, which would soon be in our past. These peaceful moments we'd cherish as we'd be moving from the area soon. Hopefully, the turmoil faded to the back of our minds.

After school began, none of us saw the Simpsons much. When we did see them at the bus stop and sometimes along the way, their demeanor expressed an awareness of our families' conflict. It usually escalated during the weekends.

My seventh-grade classroom, like a small basement with a concrete floor, was across from the school's cafeteria under an eighth-grade room. We had another Mr. Hunter. His last name was the same as my sixth-grade teacher's, but they were different people. New to the school, this Mr. Hunter's personality was much harsher than my sixth-grade Mr. Hunter's gentle one. It didn't matter that much to me; I was a good student, excited and happily awaiting the move into our new house.

On September 24, 1956, moving day finally came. With all the excitement, no one in my family wanted to go to school, but I had never missed a day. Since I would be the only one of us waiting for the school bus, Daddy drove me. Once there, time passed very slowly, and it was difficult to focus on school. At last the day ended, and I felt as I did when I was about to see all Santa Claus had brought me and so much more.

I walked the two blocks to our new home. The house was miraculous. A redbrick Cape Cod, it was set back from the road across from the builder's two-story white house. It looked gigantic compared to our former home! It was much larger and better than the white mill houses or any other place I'd ever seen African American families inhabit other than Miss Cranford's brother, Cou'n Marcus. The yard was covered with straw where real green grass would soon sprout. I walked along the graveled driveway and onto the small, brick-trimmed concrete porch.

Inside, an unforgettable smell of newness filled the air from the light-stained hardwood floors to the fresh, cream-colored paint on the walls. There were arches over a couple of doorways leading from the spacious living room to a dining room and to an adjacent hallway. Just that morning, our front room was called the house—a small multipurpose room with two beds, a dresser, a chest of drawers, and a coal and wood-burning heater. Now, there was a wood-burning fireplace with a mantel as yet undecorated. The large picture of a ship on the ocean that had hung over the fireboard was absent. I had looked at it for twelve long years, time enough for the ship to sail away on its avocado waves. Adjacent to the fireplace was a large picture window facing the street.

New and used furniture was purchased including a mahogany dining room set complete with a buffet. The dining room had a chandelier and a swinging door that led to a kitchen. There were double sinks and water that ran from a faucet. There would be no more dishpans or trips to fetch water. The spring was Hazel's now. Through a window over the sinks, I saw a spacious, straw-covered backyard and woods. A nearby branch marked part of our property line separating us from the white neighborhood beyond.

Numerous wooden cabinets were built into the top and bottoms of three walls replacing our small, single, metal Hoosier. A white electric stove against one wall put an end to carrying in wood and coal. Having a large white refrigerator, Rich would no longer need to wait for the iceman in summer. As I toured the house, smiling family members already there went almost unnoticed. I was mesmerized by the appearance of my own fulfilled dream.

Electric light switches were everywhere—not a kerosene lamp or flambo in sight. We no longer had safety concerns about the exposed flame due to a broken lamp globe. Nor did electric cords dangle across the ceilings as was the case in the few houses I'd visited. Imagine doing homework using electric lights with space enough to isolate myself from my siblings if I chose. We'd have to get used to using an electric iron and learn how to adjust temperature settings by fabric.

Off the spacious hallway where our new black-and-white TV sat in one corner, doors led to a bathroom, three bedrooms, the basement, and upstairs. The bathroom had a sink and bathtub with a shower. I had only experienced a summer's rain shower. It also had a real toilet that flushed, eliminating the need for a slop jar at night. With a new electric washer, Mo would be able to wash clothes in the basement. Although until sometime later, our clothes would still dry on a clothesline outside where fresh air was free. The day was miraculous and enchanting.

In addition to the beauty of our house, we were finally close to where Daddy spent most of his day, the barbershop. The majority of people in Belmont already knew us from school, church, Mo's family, and as Nat Littleton's children. Many families had at least one person, the father, and possibly a son or two who were regulars at Littleton's Barbershop. But since there were so many of us, our names were sometimes mistaken. I might be called Cassie, Carl might be called Dan, but everybody knew Rich for sure. We were all elated but no one as much as Daddy, who had finally achieved his goal and saw his family well pleased. It was a day of appreciation, of understood thanks, and of celebration for Daddy's victory.

In school, Clara and I enjoyed writing skits for our classmates to perform after lunch especially on bad-weather days. Our teacher allowed us to distribute strips of notebook paper with written scripts to participating students. Each skit had a purpose, and it usually involved a situation and problem-solving dilemma dealing with others in our age group. The rest of the class watched the presentations and applauded at the end. Mr. Hunter occasionally allowed a few classmates to walk home with me to prepare refreshments for a class special, after-lunch holiday party, or celebration. Everyone liked my new house.

Early December, I was sitting with my class at one of the long, rectangular tables by the wall in the cafeteria. Our teacher ate nearby with staff. The large room was crowded as it always was when we had pinto beans, coleslaw, a square of cornbread, and best of all, apple pie with a slice of mellow cheese on top. A discussion about Christmas had just begun when Clara sprang from the table.

"There's no such thing as Santa Claus," she blurted loudly. "It's your mama and daddy!"

A puzzled expression was all over my face, but I couldn't speak. I thought she had lost her mind. Was she right? How did she know? Who else knew? And why had it taken me that long to find out? Santa was the biggest, most pleasant treat ever; I wasn't ready for the secret to be ruined. I reflected on the wide, deep tracks I had seen in the snow when I was about three and a half. Until Clara's blunt announcement, those were Santa's sleigh tracks, not a large box of toys Daddy dragged to our porch.

Then I recalled the Christmas when Santa forgot baby dolls for Cassie and me. Mo saw our disappointment and allowed us to go to Joe Farrington's store to pick one out. And what about the Christmas Eve when Rich convinced me the airplane we saw was Santa and his sleigh? I had been sure he was on his way to our house. I wanted to remain sure, but how could I? Our parents were so smart and secretive like other parents I learned; they protected our excitement once a year at Christmastime. That was the one special day to receive lots of gifts we'd requested. Along with making sure we went to church to reemphasize Jesus's birth, they delighted in making us ecstatic.

While I was glad to learn the truth about Santa, I hadn't wanted to learn about it from Clara that way. Instead, I wished she had whispered that reality to me. It would've given me time to absorb all the goodness I'd experienced over the years without numerous classmates seeing my reaction. I don't even recall if I was the only one at the table who didn't know. But for sure, except for exposing the truth to Cassie, I wouldn't be the one to tell my younger siblings. I'd let them enjoy the excitement for as long as they could.

As we got older, Daddy remained adamant about education. "You can't do much in life without a good education," he'd say. "You don't give up. Things get in the way sometimes, and people get in your way too. But you get your education. That's the only way you can turn things around and not have to live like we did."

He had concerns about other issues and reminded us of certain necessary changes in our new lifestyle. "You chaps turn off some of those lights! The house is lit up like a Christmas tree! You trying to outshine the sun!"

Daddy was right: we had to get used to a lot of luxury at once after being content with so little for years. We'd been patient until the family grew so large and Hazel practically forced us to move. We were rich with family, close physically due to lack of space, but we were well nurtured and always had a sense of belonging. Having a mother who was there correcting us rather than defending us was helpful. Mo taught us there were consequences for our misbehavior; sometimes, she'd punish us or we'd learned from our own mistakes. The first twelve years of my life took place in a house of good experiences. They shaped me into the person I've become.

I knew I'd have to do my best in Mr. Hunter's class and all the others. I knew Daddy had been smart in high school while at the same time attending barbering college. Finally, he'd provided a more than adequate house for us. Daddy had accomplished his goals. All I could do at that point was remain a smart student one year at a time.

## Chapter 19

# NEW COURSES, NEW BOYS—GRADES 8–10

In eighth grade, I was in Mr. Henderson's class, the other teacher from the military. He'd come to Reid High the same year as my sixth-grade teacher had. Mr. Henderson was a good, respected teacher, smartly dressed in perfect-fitting suits; his well-groomed hair was much higher than Daddy's.

As the student population grew, school boundaries changed between Reid High and Highland High, the African American high school in Gastonia. Consequently, several of my friends and classmates left that year as they were required to attend school in that district.

My original classmates and I had English in a notoriously strict older teacher's classroom. She taught well, but she shouldn't have gotten away with how she deliberately embarrassed some students in her classes. I listened uncomfortably as she spoke without tact and commented openly on whatever personal problems students might have. I liked English and did well; in fact, it was my favorite subject. But to my mind, no amount of knowledge or teaching ability made my teacher's unprofessionalism acceptable. Neither did she deserve the respect given her possibly out of fear as several of her former students, some of my classmates, and other adults shared with me through the years.

The following year, I started high school. Student enrollment for grades one through twelve at Reid High was just over eight hundred. New students who transferred from Mount Holly added a lot of interest to the school day. Several became classmates and good friends. Others were cousins we didn't know well from both Mo's and Daddy's families. As a freshman, I found my new classmates most interesting, including the boys, as I had known the others in my class since first grade.

One boy from nearby Lowell, a small township west of Belmont, liked me and asked to escort me to the Freshman Ball. John was a well-mannered, well-respected A student in Rich's class. I wore a nice dress, low-heeled dress shoes, and stockings for the first time. John, handsomely dressed in a suit and tie, came to my house to walk me to the school gym. Mo came to the living room to meet him while several of my siblings looked on. He addressed my mother as Mrs. Littleton as if he'd had lots of practice. Though I nervously smiled as I was going out with a boy for the first time, he was at ease. He held my moist hand while walking the two blocks and handled what little conversation there was.

Gwen danced at home stepping about in her penny loafers and bobby socks, but I wasn't used to it. When my date and I danced to a slow song, it was the first time I'd experienced a male body that close to mine but with much space between. His arms around my waist and shoulder and my mixture of nerves and shyness—that was a feeling I hadn't had before.

When the ball ended, John walked me home in the dark. Holding my hands briefly in our driveway, he gave me a gentle kiss beside my mouth before walking me to my door. He was a gentleman; I was filled with flurries.

I saw John occasionally at school and was reminded of the warm connection we had shared. However, I was not ready for dating; I later learned another girl, an upperclassman, was interested in him. She eventually became his girlfriend.

Like Millie, I had joined the glee club, later called the high school chorus. Our music director was excellent, and we often won top ratings in state competitions year after year. That spring, on a Sunday afternoon, I saw small groups of unfamiliar African American teenagers strolling on the newly paved street in front of my house and around the block. Who were they? Cassie and I were curious, but we didn't venture across the yard to welcome them or ask why they had come. Later, we learned they were a high school glee club from a North Carolina city, Gramlet, about two hours away. They had arrived on a school bus to sing in their director's family church, which was right around the corner from our house.

During summer of '59, I spent a lot of time with Betty, a classmate who lived a few blocks from me. We saw each other almost daily and would giggle over anything. After finishing our chores, we walked back and forth to each other's houses sometimes picking wild plums on a vacant lot near my driveway or along the street to her house.

At times, Betty's mother called her back inside to complete an unfinished job before she slipped away for a short while. Although both of us had a television in our homes, what was there to watch during the middle of the day? We were outside often even when the sun was so hot it seemed to scorch our faces. Sometimes, we'd meet and talk with a couple other neighborhood friends or classmates. Finally, the humdrum months ended. Once school began in the fall of '59, Betty had her own group of friends and I had mine, but I still liked her as I had during the summer.

In geometry class during my sophomore year, for the first time I could remember, we were issued brand-new, crisp, clean textbooks. There were no lists of unrecognizable names as in the worn, secondhand books we'd received from the white school. Of course we would have appreciated new textbooks and new school buses as well years ago. Nevertheless, as during my early childhood, despite the inequality and separation between the two races, a way of life especially in the south, Belmont was still a nice, peaceful place to live. In the small town to my knowledge, whites and African Americans got along without much social interaction other than through jobs and businesses. I can recall pleasant experiences with whites in the stores my siblings and I frequented in North Belmont. Also, my sisters and I had had brief, friendly communication with the white Radcliff girls.

However, I can only envision myself on a hot day sitting on a stool in a café licking a cone of delectable ice cream. Rich, though, with his outgoing personality but surrounded by sisters due to his birth order, found white male friends in the Acme Mill village. They ventured into our familiar woods but not in public.

Mo had good, friendly relationships with the police officer and the women for whom she ironed in North Belmont. At least two stayed in touch with her after we'd moved. Mo had their phone numbers, and one woman occasionally dropped by to see her.

We accepted life the way it was presented to us; we evaded friction. African Americans lived in other scattered pockets in North Belmont, but there were two main small areas connecting my family: Stowe Spinning Company and Acme Spinning Company. In my new part of society closer to town, two other main African American sections were separated by downtown Belmont—the community surrounding Reid High and the one on the other side of town.

Throughout history in African American society, neighborhood churches of various denominations were our bond. Our togetherness through churches helped strengthen Belmont's African American communities. Therefore, neither separation nor inequality hindered us from striving to reach our potential. Segregation was accepted as standard and wasn't changing, but many of us proved that a good education, particularly at Reid High, would help us succeed regardless.

That day in geometry, my name was called over the intercom to leave early with the girls' basketball team for an away game.

I had made the team! My male geometry teacher didn't hide his surprise; he smiled big. Maybe he didn't think a fast-moving sport like basketball fit my personality. He was probably right; though I could shoot, I wasn't as aggressive as some of my teammates and played very little. Vigorous neighborhood basketball games with friends on a nearby vacant lot and no pressure from spectators would prove best for me.

I joined the New Homemakers of America. While my favorite subject was English, I enjoyed homemaking class. It was in the same building where that dentist had surprised me by pulling two of my teeth years earlier. There, I learned about children, family relationships, housing, food, and cooking, and so much more. Most of all, after using Mo's pedal machine for so long, I enjoyed learning to sew on the electric sewing machine. My homemaking teacher was pleased with my progress and skill in her class. She came to my house after school one day to photograph my home project, three colorful, geometric shaped pillows with piping inserted in the seams. The solid colors blended with our sofa and matched the room's décor.

My homeroom and social studies teacher was a young, tall, slender man with a heavy mustache. A classmate, Christina, and I had become close friends. Having visited friends and relatives in his city, Gastonia, she knew him a lot better than I did; she even knew his nickname. One day after lunch, Christina and I were talking by our lockers in the crowded corridor of the newest classroom building. Unlike all the other brick school buildings with gabled roofs, this one was long with a flat top. As we got books for our next classes, I called our teacher by his nickname, Gootie. Christina suddenly went deaf and asked me to repeat his name louder and louder. Finally, I stood up from my low-leveled locker and yelled, "Gootie!" just as he walked by. Christina burst out laughing as he glanced at us perhaps wondering why I had called his name. Embarrassed, I entered his class avoiding his eyes as well as Christina's smile. I was afraid it might prompt us to giggle. And since Gootie didn't mention the incident but focused on our lesson, I focused on it too.

Christina and I had many more laughs together, but we were more likely to talk about boys than about our teachers. She came to my house early on school mornings so we could walk to school together. While there was a small store near our elementary school building where students sometimes bought snacks and school supplies, we'd stop at the small corner store near my house. We'd buy two oranges or a large one for a nickel, or a huge Baby Ruth or Mr. Goodbar, ginger snaps, or other treats. Sometimes, we cautiously shared the goodies in class. Occasionally for lunch on Mondays, Christina would bring a delicious slice of pecan pie or cake her mother had made for Sunday's dinner. She shared it with me and sometimes other classmates. We were sweet buddies, best friends.

Christina had learned how to make a puppet on her hand by drawing a face on her fist and putting lipstick around the thumb and forefinger. That formed a mouth, which she made move while saying funny things. I did it too, and we laughed. She also had a funny cough that sounded like a baby's, which made several of us giggle. Christina was fun and put silly smiles on lots of faces.

Though our classes were orderly and our teachers respected, several of us found ways to communicate and have fun in class in between learning. The most common way was to discreetly pass notes on small pieces of folded paper. Sometimes the note was funny and we had to disguise our expressions and stifle our laughter. We must've been good because I don't recall getting in trouble at least not until a couple of years later.

In time, Christina and I along with three other classmates we'd known since first grade became known as the Big Five Girls. A popular group of boys became the Big Five Boys, and a smaller group of popular girls was called the Small Four. Friends who had transferred to Reid High in ninth grade from Rollins were included in the latter two groups. But while we were members of a special group, we were friendly with each other and with those not among us. We were all part of a larger body of proud African American students, the Reid High School Rams. We were like a huge family with lots of school spirit. Blue and gold were our school colors, and our teachers seemed to have a genuine interest in our success. Many of them had taught our older siblings, or shared some connection with our parents and families, or attended one of the churches in the area.

In the middle of the school year, there was a horrific event in Belmont. Our wonderful and caring principal and the assistant principal were killed in a car accident. They were both well liked and highly respected, and their deaths were a great loss to their families, the school, and our community. I had had the same principal for ten years, and I had assumed he'd always be there. The high school chorus director served as interim principal until there was a replacement.

Throughout the years, there were special events for the students' enjoyment at Reid High. On some Friday afternoons, a movie, often a western, was shown in the school gym for a small fee, and I usually went with most of my class. Occasionally, there was a talent show. But once, a magician came with fascinating tricks. He produced pieces of white, wrapped candy that were thrown for us to scramble after or catch. For some reason, we called it "cat candy." Later, I saw that same taffy in several stores without the magic.

Once, the gym was packed for a live Frankenstein show where under dim lights, the scary, quite realistic character wandered into the screaming audience. Although I knew Frankenstein was not a real monster, it was a bit eerie walking home in the dark even with family.

We students attended exciting basketball and football games, and of course, we were the best! One memorable chant declared that when a rooster was put on a fence and had to choose between the two teams, it cheered for Reid High because it had some sense.

During that year, a band from Charlotte played in the gym, and I met Walter, a handsome band member. He told me they'd soon be playing at the club next to Daddy's barbershop. My friend Betty had met the leader and saxophonist, and I pleaded with Mo to let me go.

She was concerned since mostly young adults went to that club. I was just fifteen; she felt I was too young. Mo was the one who made such decisions while Daddy worked. She finally gave in when Gwen said she would be there. Rich also offered to check on me in between shining shoes for a fee for some of Daddy's customers.

I wore a straight skirt, blouse, and casual slippers. When the band played the Crests' "Sixteen Candles," a slow love song, I just about melted. Walter, who was celebrating his sixteenth birthday that night, stared at me as he sang. I watched from the crowded, smoke-filled dance floor as a few couples began dancing. When the band took a break, Walter met me at his car, which was parked in front of the barbershop. But just as our conversation began, Rich came out to say I shouldn't be outside the club. With that, Walter headed back inside and I headed home, uncomfortable and too young to stay.

Father Andrew, a young, white priest from the abbey, chaperoned dances on Friday nights at Saint Benedict Catholic School, which we simply called the Catholic school. It was in a small building near the barbershop and no longer used as a school; it offered the only social outlet in Belmont for African American teenagers. The jukebox was filled with the latest dance music free to us as Father Andrew managed with a coin. Teenagers, often boys we knew from Rollins School and occasionally Highland High in Gastonia, where my friends and classmates attended after seventh grade, also came to socialize. They, sometimes including me, swing-danced and did the Twist, Pony, Mashed Potato, Scotch, and others. Cassie was good and caught on to new dances easily. Still somewhat shy, I enjoyed trying to learn the basics to keep up. But by the time I finally got the hang of some new dances, they were old.

During each event, Father Andrew circulated the room gently moving his body and bouncing to the upbeat rhythms. When couples danced to a slow song, he made sure they weren't too close; a simple eyeing meant farther separation was in order. Everyone was courteous with Father Andrew. We understood the dance was to be a respectful social occasion. The priest and Daddy had a friendly relationship. Once a barber himself, sometimes Father Andrew went to the barbershop for haircuts while other times he cut Daddy's hair.

That summer, there were other visitors from Gramlet. A female holiness minister came to preach. A few female members of her family and a couple of other women accompanied her. Their revival was held on weeknights under a large tent set up in a vacant lot a block from my house. Anyone who couldn't fit under the packed tent found cramped standing space just outside.

Some of the service could be heard from our front yard. Mo, hearing about Sister Robinson from us and her women friends, went only once, but Cassie and I attended several times. There was preaching, singing, clanking cymbals, and jingling tambourines. Attendants sweated, and some shouted with the Spirit of the Holy Ghost. "Thank you, Jesus! Thank you, Jesus!" they yelled. The shouting and loud music made me anxious especially when a couple of my neighborhood friends and classmates yelled out like the grown-ups. They were jumping up and down with flailing arms and fixed eyes. When neither Cassie nor I shouted, I wondered if something was wrong with us. After all, we too were emotionally stirred about the Holy Spirit. We had grown up knowing and believing in Jesus Christ. Were we withholding our spiritual feelings?

Inspired, Cassie and I agreed with several neighborhood girls to hold a prayer meeting in our basement, a spacious and private area. Each had shouted under the tent. When the youngest girl started calling out "Jesus" and jumping about and waving her arms, Cassie and I got scared. We were amazed our praying and singing had triggered such a physical and emotional outburst. Not knowing what to do or if we should do anything, we were perplexed. What if the girl hit her head on one of the metal basement poles? We waited until she settled down before our group dispersed.

Large amounts of money were collected at the Holiness Revival as Sister Robinson and one of the women who came with her continuously encouraged the crowd to give. I felt guilty having little or nothing to put in the collection plate as it passed along the row where I sat. However, I witnessed many people generously giving what appeared to be lots of money. I wondered if they had succumbed to the coaxing. Sister Robinson already drove a big, expensive Cadillac, but maybe everyone gave as his or her heart guided.

Later, I learned strict guidelines to the holiness religion forbade jewelry, makeup, and dancing. Well, Cassie and I had pierced ears and didn't want to give up our earrings though we still wore little or no makeup. And we always looked forward to going to the Friday-night dances at the Catholic school. After careful thought, we decided not to give up our Friday-night fun as did my friend Betty, an excellent dancer. At any rate, as was the case with other events, Mo determined whether Cassie and I went. Mo made sure the kitchen was cleaned and we hadn't been sassy or hardheaded. Though Mo and I did have occasional conflicts, I knew she was the boss and I needed to always respect her.

I had learned from Gwen how to straighten and curl my shoulder-length hair, which I wore with bangs and a small ponytail sometimes to the side. Or I kept it loose with a few curls combed behind my ears. But that summer, I wanted a new look, something short and fashionable. So early on a Tuesday morning, a light business day for Daddy, I went to the barbershop. Trusting him, I didn't look in the mirror even after he'd finished. I just smiled and left. But when I got outside and felt the back of my head, there was nothing there! *Did he cut off all my hair?* I felt almost bald. I was anxious. I took the shortcut, a path between houses along the street, home to examine my hair in the mirror. To my relief, I loved the new style. It was short, tapered, and neatly squared at the back of my neck. A short part on the right side formed bangs to the left. My family and friends loved it too; they filled my day with compliments. One expressed how becoming the style was and how it accented my facial features. Not only did I have a new chic look, but it would also be easier to manage than longer-length hair. Daddy knew what he was doing, but he still wouldn't cut Mo's hair. Years earlier, he had let her know he preferred her hair long. So she learned to do it herself—cutting bangs and leaving the rest shoulder length and shorter. The ends curled up, so if she made any mistakes, they weren't noticeable.

The summer was a time to feel free and creative. Cassie sewed too. We began making simple clothing for ourselves as well as doing clothing repair to earn some spending money. We made simple skirts, usually A-line or pleated, cotton popover tops, and culottes much of which we wore to Stowe Park on Tuesdays. We bought fabric, a new priority over snacks, at a textile store down hot Highway 74. Fabric became our new term for what we had before simply called cloth.

Much more hot pavement surrounded our new home than in the Acme Mill area. Unlike our barefooted younger siblings, Cassie and I wore shoes unless we were in our grassy yard. We were carefree in sandals, shorts, and tops.

After learning in class how to follow a simple store-bought pattern in our dining room, I began making more-complex outfits to wear to church. Sometimes, I started early on Saturday to be ready for Sunday. I'd stay up late to finish a dress or matching skirt and top. I eventually learned sewing was less tiring if I did all the pinning and cutting at least a day before. I also learned I should've removed Mo's white lace dining room tablecloth before cutting. Before I knew it, I thought, *Oops! I've cut a big gash through the lace along with my pattern and fabric.* Mo didn't seem to notice the damage until after the linen was washed. Then, the clean-cut scissor's path had been altered. In time, another white cloth covered the table. (Just recently, Cassie told me she had made the same mistake, and we laughed.)

My chores were easier compared to what they'd been at our other house, so other than Stowe Park and the Friday night dances, summer was boring. What jobs could African American teenagers get? Filling in for a couple of neighborhood girls, I babysat in the white section near town. Each time, the children left to play nearby. For one young boy, I hadn't been alerted or prepared for such behavior, and I had no phone number to call his mother. Even if I did, how alarming it would be to call to say, "I can't find your child"? Neither did I feel comfortable going into the unfamiliar, white neighborhood searching for him. The boy, however, was smart enough to return home before his mother did.

In the other case, I did have a phone number but luckily spotted the young, adorable brother and sister next door and brought them home. I liked them a lot and babysat another day. After that, I decided those babysitting jobs were not for me; they were too risky and the pay was too little. In hindsight, I concluded that since I was just filling in, the first parent had forgotten to give me necessary information regarding her son's safety. I hadn't thought to ask. As a babysitter, safety should've been the priority, more important than washing dishes, dusting, or ironing clothes, which were expected in addition to caring for the child.

Later though, in my neighborhood, I babysat several times for two cousins closely related to Miss Cranford. Although the pay was even less than for the white children, as with the young brother and sister, the experience was rewarding. (I hardly saw the first boy). I'd enjoyed watching the two delightful children play and interact with one another while talking in their soft voices. On the other hand, the cousins were adorable babies. And since they were not yet walking, I was in total control of their needs and safety. Not once was I asked to do more than that.

As a family trip, my parents took most of us not to Myrtle Beach but to Atlantic Beach. It was the only beach for African Americans in the Carolinas. I was in awe when I saw the ocean for the first time. As beautiful as it was when I watched the waves come and go, splashing on the sand and my feet, I began to feel uncomfortable in the large crowd. After having marveled at the seemingly endless body of water, much later, I had other thoughts and questions. I couldn't imagine a wall high and thick enough to keep African Americans on their side. Yes, there was a swimming pool for us in

Gastonia and numerous whites-only swimming pools, but the ocean too? Were we that inferior? Though He parted the sea, God surely didn't divide His beautiful ocean so whites could have a separate section of their own. Just being on the beach, socializing, feeling the sand on their feet, swimming, wading, gazing at the vast ocean, and hearing the unique sounds of its waves would bring African Americans back. But since Myrtle Beach wasn't open to us, we had no other choice. Was it different? I had no doubt that it must be better for whites.

At that time, I took for granted nothing would ever change simply because things had always been that way. Later, I realized it would take lots of African Americans to make life equal and fair for us, but who would go first?

## Chapter 20

# POPULARITY, BOYFRIENDS, AND GRADUATION—GRADES 11-12

It was 1960, and Rich had gotten his driver's license. On some Sunday afternoons, he borrowed Daddy's Oldsmobile and took Cassie and me to the swimming pool in Gastonia. In time, I met Harold, a handsome, popular lifeguard who attended Highland High.

Later that summer, he came to the Friday night Catholic school dance with a couple of his friends. One was interested in Cassie while the other friend showed an interest in our cousin Katie, Mr. Ezell's daughter (he'd brought our dry cleaning). Harold was a good dancer, but there were two problems that prevented us from dating: communication and transportation. It would be a while before Daddy felt we could afford a telephone. Therefore, to make and receive calls, I used my cousins' phone a couple of houses away. Also, with no car of his own, Harold could come to Belmont only when he got a ride with a friend. Though I saw him now and then, he'd let me know when he and a friend would be coming to Stowe Park. There, we'd meet on the dance floor, talk, and dance. However, for the most part, we remained disconnected.

Daddy continued to bring home watermelons he would stash on our dining room floor leaving some in his barbershop. But in late fall, he brought home a couple of dozen large, double-yolk eggs that some of us didn't want to eat. I didn't know what kind of chicken had laid them or if they were even from a chicken. After dark on a very cold evening, my neighbor, who was attending a nearby college, and I hid several eggs in our coat pockets. As we walked around the block laughing like crazy, we slammed a number of eggs on our neighbors' concrete porches. On my way to school the next morning, the eggs were frozen and a couple of neighbors appeared to have difficulty sweeping them away. That part I had not anticipated, but I played innocent, smiling and greeting them as I tamed my laughter. Fortunately, my friend and I weren't caught. Probably the neighbors thought some young mischievous boys, or even Rich, were responsible for our prank.

Since activities for African American teenagers were limited in Belmont, roller-skating became a fun activity that winter. Metal roller skates were attached to the soles of our shoes, the clamps tightened with a special key. Wearing heavy coats and head coverings, we skated on the street in front of the school sometimes forming a train by holding on to each other at their waists from behind. A long line of us roared down the asphalt. As cold as it was, it took no time for our bodies to warm. Skating back and forth, we perspired as if we had run for miles.

There was a little problem, however; I hadn't mastered maneuvering my feet to stop as Cassie and the others had. Therefore, whenever I skated alone, I had to slow down or run into a curb or a person. On the street adjacent to my house, it was exhilarating to coast down a rather steep hill knowing that it continued upward and would allow me to slow to a stop. Skating in our basement with siblings, the concrete was very smooth with tall poles to help me stop.

Junior year was memorable for many reasons. By then, I had a reputation as a good seamstress. I enjoyed making a few black shirtwaist dresses including my own for the high school chorus members. The dresses had gathered waists and buttoned bodices.

When one of our chorus performances was televised, the director took notice. At his request, I stepped out front to display my dress for the TV camera. I became a debutante for Alpha Kappa Alpha Sorority, and Harold invited me to his high school's junior prom in Gastonia. I was excited to spend special time with him again especially at that beautiful event.

Harold was a popular football player and was smart and respectful. I really liked him and wanted to get to know him better. Unfortunately, too much time between communicating with each other kept us apart. I wondered what might have been if we had actually dated.

Our chorus received another top rating at a state competition in Greensboro, a little more than two hours away. Afterward, a nice boy I knew from Rich's class sat beside me on the bus home. When I wasn't napping, we had a pleasant conversation in the dark. He talked about dating me, but no sooner had we become somewhat familiar with each other than he joined the navy. We wrote each other, and he sent a nice picture of himself in uniform.

That summer, my math teacher taught me drivers' education, and while I did well, I wasn't in a hurry to get my license; I didn't have a car. By then, Rich was making plans to attend barbering college in Winston-Salem, North Carolina, that September. The family shared his excitement as he was going to be a barber just like our daddy.

Mo was proud of me. She too had become more sociable after moving close to longtime friends and relatives and meeting our neighbors. With increased social interactions, she toughened a bit and would speak up when it came to expressing her feelings. She became an usher in church and a member of the ladies' auxiliary. Daddy was a Mason, so as his wife, she became a member of the Eastern Star. For years, Daddy had been the church steward who collected and counted the money. He also found members to have the preacher and his family for dinner on Sundays, us included.

Daddy still enjoyed eating supper outside on pleasant days just as he had on the big rock in front of our previous home. One evening, he sat eating at the end of our graveled driveway near the back of our house. I stood nearby at an elaborate, concrete fishpond Mo had created. She had embellished it with ferns, monkey grass, and colorful flowers along with various-sized goldfish.

Between bites, Daddy once again began to talk about his military experiences. As a child, I had not understood the political ramifications relating to the war. Neither did I understand how far away from home Daddy had been, nor how his duties in West Germany had contributed to the war. I didn't recall ever hearing him tell his story to the rest of the family, though I assumed he had. His experiences during World War II and my birth were connected; I was his reminder.

"You know, Maggie took the chaps," he said. "Went and stayed with Gernie and Pete." He scooped his food. "Your mama was expecting you."

Nodding to confirm I was listening, I said, "Yes sir, I remember."

As if for the first time, he continued to tell the story while he ate stewed potatoes, slimy stewed okra cooked only for him, steak fish, and sliced tomatoes, which we always had in the summer. Occasionally he glanced up maybe to see if my facial expression showed I understood the anguish he was reliving. I did; I was his almost grown-up daughter interested in knowing the struggles he and other African Americans in the military had encountered.

Daddy said they were treated like second-class citizens while in Germany just as we were treated in America. I had never known any other way. Since that was the way of life for us, unfair laws and all, how would our lives ever get better? Being a democratic nation didn't help us get fair treatment. In fact, Aunt Lydia even had a picture of slaves she had known working the fields. They too had helped build America.

It seemed Daddy had mistakenly thought that by being in the U.S. military, African Americans would be exempted from

mistreatment and all soldiers would be considered equal. That was not so. Whites often mistreated him and other black soldiers. When Mo learned of this in Daddy's letters from Germany, she like many others felt it was appalling, though I'd learn this much later. The men were there for the same purpose—to serve the U.S. Army. But Daddy was used to prejudice only back at home in America and did not expect it in Germany. By risking his life for his country, he probably thought the deal for justice in return was understood. Nevertheless, though it appeared Daddy had more to say, it seemed he'd learned the hard way in the army.

My neighborhood friend Betty and I had begun to straighten and curl hair for a few women in their homes. We charged a reasonable fee, and our customers seemed satisfied. One of the women was very light skinned with reddish-brown hair that proved my undoing. One day as I loosened the cheap curling iron I'd overheated on a hot plate, one of her curls stuck and was burned to a crisp. Boy was I shocked. As I scraped the almost unidentifiable hair from the hot curler, she thankfully understood. Nevertheless, Daddy told me I had to stop the unlicensed business. He said I was taking customers from our cousin's beauty parlor at the end of his building, which Daddy owned. As the daughter of a barber, that didn't look good, so I obeyed.

Each year before school began, my siblings and I got new school clothes. That year, the shopping was different. In the early fall of 1961, for the first time, Daddy took Cassie and me shopping in one of the large, sophisticated department stores in downtown Charlotte. The store was huge and fancy compared to the one in Gastonia and made the even smaller store where we frequented in Belmont seem tiny. We shopped for hours buying socks, shoes, undergarments, skirts, and sweaters.

Meanwhile, I was getting older and learning new things about myself. I grew up thinking of myself as shy maybe because I'd been labeled that. But in high school, I realized I was shy only around boys. There were several including my classmates or Rich's who expressed their interest in me through discreet messages from their friends. However, for the yearbook, a senior snapshot was taken of a handsome, respectful classmate, Larry, and me. We sat together hand in hand on a low wall outside the main classroom building. In cap and gown, our photographs were placed side by side as a couple.

Larry once came to the Catholic school on a Friday night, and we danced to a romantic song. These boys like my longtime classmates mostly from Rollins School were all nice and respectful. I liked them too. Nevertheless, we never became boyfriend and girlfriend. I was too shy to let them know I was interested in them; I expected males to express their interest in me first, but they all seemed shy as well—after all, they hadn't approached me directly.

Millie's and Gwen's dates and boyfriends quickly learned how strict Daddy was with his girls; he meant business. And any boyfriend I had needed to respect me, not just Daddy. Harold and I no longer communicated. Though Daddy had gotten us a phone, there were still nine miles between Belmont and Gastonia. I assumed Harold had a girlfriend at his high school, and why wouldn't he?

During my senior year, several of the boys in my class became school bus drivers just like Tommy Dunn to whom I'd written that love letter in third grade. What was I thinking?

That last year at Reid High, I experienced my first steady boyfriend. William, the only student I knew who had his own car, was from Rollins School. He was very well dressed, neat, handsome and, most important, respectful. Once, he took me to his home where his parents were very welcoming. Another time we went to a What-a-Burger in Belmont and sat under the lights in his shiny, turquoise-and-white Buick. I could have choked trying to keep him from hearing me chew the crispy iceberg lettuce on the burger.

He took me to Reid High's senior prom. My class of '62 and our guests had fun dancing to the theme "Under the Magnolias." I wore a pink, below-the-knee dress I'd made. All in satin, it was sleeveless with a plain bodice and full gathered skirt. A wide sash hung down the back. I also made a prom dress of yellow satin with yellow chiffon overlay for one of my classmates.

By that time, I was more outgoing. I was an attendant for the Queen of Roses Ball and had been secretary and assistant secretary. I was a member of the French Club, the Blue and Gold Staff (in charge of compiling the yearbook), and student council representative.

A few friends said my various hairstyles were very becoming. Occasionally, I'd change the part from the side to the middle for a different look, and I loved *Vogue* fashions. Also, I was articulate and had confidence to speak before the student body during a program. Knowing this, even though at home I was still pulling out a few eyelashes now and then, a couple of classmates suggested I try modeling. While I was flattered, I couldn't imagine a future in such a career.

My real ambition was to become an English teacher. I'd always enjoyed the subject and had long contemplated that as my college major. Like a couple of my classmates, I had good penmanship, and our teacher and senior class advisor often asked me to write assignments on the blackboard. Sometimes, I took charge at the board diagraming sentences while the class participated. It was like a fun game to me; it was oddly similar to working with fractions.

When my chemistry teacher left me in charge of his class, I found it intriguing, but it never crossed my mind to major in chemistry or science, interesting subjects. I couldn't see beyond being able to teach English. As far as I knew, all African American graduates interested in education became teachers.

During the last several days of my senior year, my classmates and I realized we probably would be ending our boyfriend-girlfriend relationships. Some of us planned to leave for various colleges. After lunch in the cafeteria, I socialized outside with mostly the Big Five girls. We sat in the sun along a brick ledge between the long classroom building and cafeteria listening to a classmate's transistor radio.

As Chuck Jackson's love song "Any Day Now" played, my

sentimental friends and I displayed sad faces that matched the lyrics. A few tears were shed though I couldn't squeeze any out. If the class bell hadn't rung, several of the girls probably would've become pitiful, sobbing messes especially if James Brown's "Lost Someone" had played.

Throughout my childhood, my father had always emphasized the importance of a good education for all eight of his children. My two older sisters chose marriage over college though I never heard Daddy express any disappointment. Mo expressed the same wish for us to further our education but in a different way. She was the one who read every report card and signed them happily or with concern and alerted us to the possible consequences. She was the one who made sure we did homework and knew when we needed to complete assignments, but in most cases, we didn't need coaxing. My report cards had been good for as long as I could remember.

In 1962, I graduated third in my small class of forty-three students. Instead of the A or B I'd expected, I'd received a C in a class for talking and unsuccessfully attempting to pass a note. Neither the talking nor the note had anything to do with my academic ability, but the C dropped me from second to third in my class and caused me to fall short of the salutatorian criteria. It also affected my belief in that teacher's honesty and fairness as a professional, but in time, I was forgiving. I planned on grading with integrity and fairness when I become a teacher.

I applied for a National Defense Student Loan. Father Andrew assisted me in completing the application, and I was approved. Later, I thought the two girls with the higher averages may not have qualified for it. Maybe they would've qualified only for a scholarship.

For a long time, I'd known I would somehow attend college; I was sure my future depended on it. I, along with the two top students and two other classmates, all my friends, chose the same college just three hours away. Despite having decided to attend North Carolina College at Durham (later North Carolina Central University), I still wasn't sure what I would study. No matter what major I chose, I'd always need good language skills. I knew one day I'd write even if just as a hobby, and put my story on paper as a record for my present and future family. I knew I'd write about my childhood, my family, and the little house where the towering chinaberry tree stood. I'd tell about the fun we'd had exploring nature and going to the spring where cool water flowed. I'd write about Hazel, who I assumed still lived there though I couldn't imagine her having a neighbor; we'd worn that house out. However, I don't recall any particular damage, but any new tenant would have had to be in dire need of shelter or a place to hide to want to live there.

In high school, I'd enjoyed the various home economics subjects and felt there was a lot more to learn. Despite having considered majoring in English, I chose home economics with a minor in education. As I said, I knew all along I'd be a teacher. What other profession was there for African American women? The neighbor on one side of my house was the school's librarian. A first-grade teacher lived on the other side, across the street lived a high school English teacher (her husband had built our house), and a third-grade teacher lived on the next street around the corner. Additionally, several relatives were teachers, including Miss Cranford and a cousin closely related to Aunt Lydia. They and all the others who had taught at my all African American schools for twelve years were my role models.

When it was time for my boyfriend, William, to go to a different North Carolina college about two hours away, I was invited to ride with him and his mother. After a short stay, we dropped him off at his dormitory, and he and I said our private good-byes. I knew he'd get to know many girls, possibly one or two becoming his girlfriends. I knew I'd meet other boys at my college. William's mother was pleasant, but I was shy around her simply because she was his mother. I just hope I said something to her on the long trip back without him.

Following high school graduation, Daddy continued to encourage me to get my driver's license. By then, Rich had graduated from barbering school. He would complete his apprenticeship with Daddy and had already purchased his first car, a navy-blue '62 Ford Galaxy.

Knowing I could drive his car, I agreed to get my license. Rich wasn't a very good role model though. Once, he ran up on a curb damaging his front bumper. He knew Daddy would be upset thinking his son was a reckless driver. Just as in his younger days, Rich needed our help. When Daddy questioned the damage, Rich said he had swerved to avoid hitting a little white dog, a very caring gesture. I'd agree if asked as that was exactly what Rich had already told me. As children, he had taught us how to discern what should be revealed regarding his mischief and how to be loyal to a brother and help him evade trouble with our parents. Now, the entire family knows the tale about that little white dog Rich hadn't hit.

By that time, Daddy had gone from a Ford to an Oldsmobile to a Buick. One Sunday, he took the passenger seat of his two-tone green sedan letting me drive the family the short distance to church. Being extra cautious, according to Daddy, I waited much too long to make a left turn onto O'Conner's Grove's driveway after yielding to an oncoming car.

"Tricie Ann," Daddy shouted, "you could've been made that turn! That car was way down the road!"

Just like Mo, I never drove with Daddy in his car again.

Occasionally on Sunday afternoons, Rich let me drive his car to take Cassie, a few friends, and cousins to the swimming pool. Each time, I saw Harold, my old lifeguard friend from my sophomore and junior years. He was friendly but always on duty without much time for conversation. On the way back, we'd stop at the very popular Tony's in Gastonia for a really special treat, ice cream.

I was still receiving graduation gifts that would be useful in college such as a skirt rack from the nearby third-grade teacher. (I still have it.) Mo was proud that I wanted to become a teacher, and she made sure I had all I needed to take to college. A few times during the summer, Daddy said something to me about taking college seriously and the importance of a good education, but I was used to hearing that from him.

As departure time neared, I became a bit anxious about leaving home for the first time, registering for classes, finding my way around campus, and settling into a dormitory. Who would be my roommate? What was her hometown? I found comfort in knowing a few friends and classmates from Reid High would be there with me.

As I packed my suitcases and footlocker for college, Daddy came to me with serious eyes.

"Tricie Ann, don't let anybody hand you any wooden nickels."

"Yes sir."

I wasn't exactly sure what Daddy was implying, but I took it to mean be careful even though I had chosen a good, reputable college. It was also well known for its school of law. As a new phase of my life was about to begin, I anxiously wondered about those wooden nickels. What did Daddy really mean? Would I be able to handle adversity with dignity? Would just being careful be good enough? His perseverance in building a spectacular house for our family came to fruition because he had never let go of his plan. But what would be my victory?

We talked no more about my education. The day for Rich to drive me to NCC's campus had at last arrived. His soon-to-be wife, Carolyn, and Mo came along, the Galaxy tightly packed and riding low.

# THE CHINABERRY TREE

Standing tall upon the slope, summer heat is blistering while countless leaves are shade.

A wire clothesline attached. A twisting rope's on the largest branch.

The lazy rides in swing of tire. Bare feet drag the red-clay ground.

Colors of fall send hearts aglow. Abandoned swing now hangs below.

Statuesque tree in winter's chill. Golden-tan berries dimpled-filled, grape-like clusters go nowhere. The art against the clear blue sky awaits spring flowers purple, white.

Fresh green berries, beads to string, girls to wear or slingshots fling. On hands the bitter taste lingers.

Summer returns with swing of tire. Colors of fall send hearts aglow. Leafless branches, golden-tan berries, the art against the clear blue sky.

Flowers, berries, countless leaves, a shady peace and endless hope. The tree stands tall upon the slope.

—Patricia L. Bostic

# ACKNOWLEDGEMENTS

First, I thank my mother for sharing family history and tales that greatly contributed to my writing this memoir. The numerous talks we had were enlightening and encouraging, while her gentle, caring nature made me want to emulate the lady she was. I appreciate my father's unique, personal connection of the war with my birth, contrasting sad and happy, his example of perseverance, as well as his emphasis on a good education for his children. I am thankful for my siblings' contributions. While many personal and humorous experiences, particularly those of my oldest brother, were shared as a family, they in various ways affected my childhood. They added spice and relevance to my life in our chinaberry hill area and, therefore, to my story.

I thank my daughter, as well as Judett Black, and Madeline Reid, who gave me objective, detailed feedback after reading my manuscript.

I greatly appreciate Leslie David Hutchens of Matthews Public Library in my current hometown. He was extremely patient and knowledgeable when assisting me with various computer skills. Leslie enabled me to submit various scheduled phases of my project in a timely manner. Early on, Ethel Aaron was also helpful and appreciated.

I am thankful for Clyde Foust and Chandra Peak of Foust Photo for photo restoration of the cover picture, my mother and me.

I thank Tamika Cobbs and Sakia Manning of Fed-Ex, who were helpful in adjusting other possible cover images.

I appreciate Reverend Charles Reid's support. He is the grandson of Reid High School's first principal, the late Charles Jesse Bynum Reid. I am grateful for the award I received in 2019 for my recollection of experiences and writing about Reid High School.

Thanks to members of the Belmont Historical Society for their support and helpful information about our hometown. To all the Gaston County business individuals in Belmont and Gastonia, who took the time to prepare a notarized permission letter for me to use various official names in my memoir, I am grateful. Factious names would have been unfitting.

I thank Helena Guiles and Paul Bruchon of our Charlotte Writers' Club Poetry Critique Group for constructive criticism and comments for my poem, The Chinaberry Tree.

Thanks to CanDee Butler of i-CanDee Photography for her understanding and patience when creating my picture gallery and headshot.

Lastly, though especially important, before committing to my publisher, I was fortunate to have obtained an editor, Annie Maier, whose professionalism and understanding matched my writing needs perfectly, just when I needed her.

Printed in the United States
by Baker & Taylor Publisher Services